Grammar to Go

Second Edition

Grammar to Go

Barbara Goldstein
Hillsborough Community College

Jack Waugh
Hillsborough Community College

Karen Linsky
Hillsborough Community College

Houghton Mifflin Company
Boston New York

Publisher: Patricia A. Coryell
Editor in Chief: Suzanne Phelps Weir
Sponsoring Editor: Joann Kozyrev
Senior Development Editor: Judith Fifer
Editorial Associate: Peter Mooney
Senior Project Editor: Margaret Park Bridges
Associate Manufacturing Buyer: Brian Pieragostini
Executive Marketing Manager: Annamarie Rice
Marketing Assistant: Andrew Whitacre

Cover image: © Thomas Barwick/Getty Images

Printed in the U.S.A.

Library of Congress Control Number: 2005934057

Instructor's exam copy:
ISBN-10: 0-618-73156-3
ISBN-13: 978-0-618-73156-5

For orders, use student text ISBNs:
ISBN-10: 0-618-63948-9
ISBN-13: 978-0-618-63948-9

3 4 5 6 7 8 9-CRW-10 09 08 07

Contents

Chapter 3 **Adjectives and Adverbs**   **30**

Chapter 4 **Phrases**   **42**

Part 2 **Handbook**   **103**

Preface

We are so pleased with *Grammar to Go*'s success and delighted to have the opportunity to make a great text even better with a second edition. We began the first edition with our belief that while simply learning grammar rules will not make a student a great writer, having a fundamental knowledge of English grammar, including the parts of speech, parts of sentences, and basic sentence construction, will give a student the tools to begin writing on a college level.

This second edition continues to present a clear, systematic, yet thorough approach to teaching English grammar to beginning college students, but it includes more opportunities for students to practice their newly acquired grammar skills through composition exercises. In addition, we have added a new feature—Word Watchers—a brief lesson on word choice at the end of each chapter to aid students as they begin to write. In addition to giving tips for spelling some commonly misspelled words like *separate* and *occasion*, the Word Watchers sections help students differentiate between confusing pairs, like *effect* and *affect* and *bad* and *badly*. Some Word Watchers lessons focus on style issues, such as sexist language and tone. Each Word Watchers lesson includes a practice set.

We have also altered the chapter order in Part 2, focusing first on the grammar issues like sentence parameters and punctuation that reinforce the lessons on clauses, which conclude Part 1. Finally, while we are philosophically opposed to providing answers in the back of the text, we have included a Test Yourself feature for each chapter, with answers provided, to enable students to check their understanding of the material. We have also provided the answer key to the Word Watchers practice sets.

Approach

Grammar to Go gives students the opportunity to learn through a step-by-step, interactive approach that minimizes memorizing rules out of context. Instead, the text incorporates pertinent information when students need it to understand the material they are studying. The book uses small, incremental steps to move from simple concepts to more complex ones. Part 1 teaches how the English language works, providing a foundation for the conventions of usage explained in Part 2. Seeing the complete picture gives students the tools to analyze their own writing from a grammatical perspective. With every step in this process, *Grammar to Go* provides reinforcement and encouragement.

Content and Organization

Chapter 1 supplies students with the basic terminology—the parts of speech and the parts of the sentence—that they need to navigate the remainder of the text. Chapter 2 presents the five basic sentence patterns as the building blocks of the English language, moving from the simplest subject/verb pattern to the more complex patterns containing complements. Chapter 3 adds single-word modifiers to the basic sentence patterns. Chapters 4 and 5 add phrases to the patterns, starting with simple prepositional phrases and moving to the more complex verbals and verbal phrases. Chapter 6 reinforces the patterns, showing that they remain the same even when word order changes. Chapters 1 through 6 prepare students to understand the complex concepts of clauses presented in Chapters 7 and 8. Part 1 ends with "Types of Sentences," reinforcing all of the concepts mastered in the first portion of the book.

Part 2 addresses specific writing issues, putting them into the grammatical framework learned in Part 1. Students are able to apply these concepts to their own writing because they now understand how the language works. For this second edition of the text, we have altered the order of the lessons in Part 2. We begin with Chapter 9 on sentence fragments and run-on sentences, directly building on the lessons of Chapters 7 and 8, which examine clauses as they expand into compound and complex sentences. Chapter 10, covering comma placement, and Chapter 11, reviewing other punctuation, also present concepts that require an understanding of phrases, clauses, and sentence types. The remaining chapters on agreement, pronouns, modifiers, and sentence coherence are now approachable; they simply build on the lessons of the previous chapters. Part 2 ends with a comprehensive reference and review chapter on parts of speech. Parts 1 and 2 progress in small steps, providing encouragement at every stage of the learning process. Unlike many traditional texts that offer exercises only at the end of large sections and chapters, *Grammar to Go* includes level-appropriate exercises at every step, checking student mastery and providing feedback.

Features

The chapters in *Grammar to Go* offer the following features:

Practice Sets: These exercises, which follow every concept presented, give students the opportunity to check their mastery of the lesson.

Quick Tips: These easily identifiable boxes offer students mnemonic devices, shortcuts, and other hints to simplify various grammatical concepts.

Composition Clues: These appropriately placed suggestions are specifically related to the writing process.

Composition Practices: The practices offer students opportunities to compose their own sentences modeled on the lessons learned in each chapter.

Parts of Speech Boxes: Parts of speech boxes present explanations of parts of speech when appropriate in the lesson.

Test Yourself: These practice sets, provided in each chapter, allow students to check their understanding of the material presented. Answers are provided in the back of the text.

Word Watchers: The minilessons at the end of each chapter focus on confusing pairs, frequently misspelled words, and language and tone. Each includes a practice set, with answers provided in the back of the text.

Grammar to Go uses a new approach to a traditional way to understand grammar. Reed and Kellogg diagramming, a system developed in the late 1800s, was a staple of teaching English grammar for three-quarters of a century. The new millennium is seeing a resurgence in this century-old system of understanding how sentences work. Diagramming is learning by doing, allowing a hands-on examination of the connections involved in constructing a sentence. It lets students visualize the relationship among sentence parts as it breaks down complicated sentences into simple, easy-to-see segments. It does not replace the study of grammar; it enhances it.

   Grammar to Go introduces diagramming in three early chapters—"Sentence Patterns," "Adjectives and Adverbs," and "Phrases"—as a way to help students visualize basic sentence patterns. We have strategically placed the diagramming instructions so that instructors who choose not to use these sections can do so without destroying the integrity of the text.

Ancillary Material

Instructor's Resource Manual. The instructor's manual continues to contain learning objectives, key terms, teaching suggestions, and additional chapter review exercises. It contains an answer key to the exercises found in the text, as well as an answer key for the additional chapter review exercises specific to the manual.

   New to the second edition is an expanded "how to" section for diagramming. Many users have told us how much the diagramming in the first four chapters has added to the learning process for their students and how they wished they were able to continue the diagramming lessons through clauses. The instructor's manual now includes a step-by-step explanation of the diagramming process for verbals, word order variations, clauses, and types of sentences, plus added diagramming exercises for instructors who wish to carry the process beyond instruction provided by the main text.

Acknowledgments

Many thanks to our students, especially the hundreds of students in various English classes at Hillsborough Community College, Dale Mabry Campus, Tampa, Florida, who used this text in its many incarnations. Their suggestions and encouragement have been invaluable.

Thanks also to those who reviewed our manuscript, and especially to one reviewer whose suggestions on passive voice have been taken seriously by us. We would also like to extend our thanks to the following reviewers for all of their suggestions and ideas:

Roy Bond, Richland College
Ruth Callahan, Glendale Community College
Christine L. Channer, Utica College of Syracuse University
Mary Jean Gilligan, Delaware Technical and Community College
Roy Neil Graves, University of Tennessee at Martin
Timothy J. Jones, Oklahoma City Community College
Patsy Krech, University of Memphis
Janene Lewis, Huston-Tillotson College
Janice S. Trollinger, Fort Valley State University
Michelle Zollars, Patrick Henry Community College

A special thanks to Lisa Kimball, our senior sponsoring editor, for her encouragement and to Judith Fifer, our development editor, for her constant perseverance.

Finally, thanks to our spouses, Bruce, Lynda, and Michael, for their support and optimism, and to other family members and our many friends, whose names appear in exercises throughout the book.

Part 1

English Grammar

Chapter 1

Getting Started

Grammar to Go is a book that will help you learn English grammar in a fast and logical way. You will process information in small, simple steps that will help you to learn some of the concepts that you may have found difficult to learn in the past.

To master English grammar, start by learning some basic terms and some simple rules. These elements will help you understand the way language works. In this "Getting Started" chapter, you will become familiar with the eight parts of speech, learn about and practice finding the subject and verb in a sentence, and see how parts of speech become parts of a sentence.

Consider this situation: A new professional football coach stands in front of his seventy-five potential players for the first time. Before he can field this team, he must learn some important lessons about them. He knows that there are several different kinds of players, each type called by a different name like tackle, end, receiver, or quarterback. He also knows that each player has a specific job to do on the field. The coach must learn who does what before he can put a single play together.

Think of grammar as the game of football. You are the coach. Your "players" are the eight parts of speech. Each one has a specific name and function. In football, there are times when some players can play different positions. For example, a tackle may become a receiver when there is a turnover. Likewise, a part of speech may serve different functions in a sentence. As you work through this book, you will see how using grammar compares with fielding a football team. First, meet your "players," the parts of speech.

Parts of Speech

Nouns

Nouns are words that name persons, places, things, or ideas. Notice the six nouns in the following sentences:

Julia played *tennis.*

Safety became a *concern.*

Mr. Todd lives in *London.*

Julia, Mr. Todd, and *London* are called **proper nouns.** Proper nouns name specific persons, places, things, or ideas. They start with capital letters.

Common nouns, like *tennis, safety,* and *concern,* do not begin with capital letters unless they begin a sentence.

The words *a, an,* and *the* are **articles,** and they always signal that a noun will follow.

I ate *a pickle.*

They had *an argument.*

The information seems important.

Other words may come between *a, an,* or *the* and the noun.

I ate *a sour pickle.*

They had *a terrible argument.*

The new information seems important.

Many nouns appear without *a, an,* or *the.*

I ate *dinner.*

They had *problems.*

Information comes from many sources.

PRACTICE SET 1–1

Directions: Underline the nouns in the following sentences.

Example: Sundari finally found her way to the station.

1. John Dover bought a digital camera.

2. Safety became a concern after the accident.

3. Owen took a job in Georgia.

4. A nervous witness sometimes forgets details.

5. The parents stayed for the refreshments.

Pronouns

A **pronoun** is a word that takes the place of a noun. Notice how pronouns replace some of the nouns in the following sentences:

Julia plays tennis.	*She* plays tennis.
Safety became a concern.	*It* became a concern.
Mr. Todd lives in London.	*He* lives in London.

These words that substitute for specific persons, places, or things are **personal pronouns.** They are the most common pronouns. Other personal pronouns include *I, me, we, us, you, him, her, they,* and *them.*

Another common type of pronoun is the **indefinite pronoun.** Indefinite pronouns include words like *each, everyone, everybody, anyone, somebody, both, some, all,* and *most.* Look at these sentences that contain indefinite pronouns:

Everyone bought a ticket.

The party caught *both* of the workers by surprise.

Anybody can learn English grammar.

PRACTICE SET 1–2

Directions: Underline all the pronouns in the following sentences. Over each one write "P" for personal pronoun or "I" for indefinite pronoun.

Example: Anyone may take him to soccer practice.

1. She gave both of the dogs a bath.

2. It really does not affect someone like me.

3. He is a better actor than anyone on the stage.

4. They surprised everyone by naming Jude to succeed her.

5. You have completed all of the assignments.

Verbs

Verbs are words that show action or state of being. They also indicate the time that the action or state of being occurs: either present, past, or future.

Look at the verbs that show action in the following sentences:

Action in the present: The spider *weaves* a web.

Action in the past:	The spider *wove* a web during the night.
Action in the future:	The spider *will weave* a new web after the storm.

Verbs like *am, is, are, was, were, seem, feel,* and *become* usually express a state of being. These verbs are called **linking verbs.**

Look at the linking verbs that show state of being in the following sentences:

State of being in the present:	I *am* tired.
State of being in the past:	After my workout, I *became* very weak.
State of being in the future:	I *will be* strong tomorrow.

PRACTICE SET 1–3

Directions: In the following sentences, underline all the verbs twice. Write "A" for action or "L" for linking over each underlined verb. On the blank, indicate whether the verb shows present, past, or future time.

          L

Example: Gary <u>seemed</u> moody.   *past* _____

1. Volcanoes erupt in many parts of the world.   _____

2. Some people are always late.   _____

3. Glass littered the street after the accident.   _____

4. Eventually, coal will become diamonds.   _____

5. The carton contains orange juice.   _____

Adjectives

Adjectives are words that describe nouns or pronouns. Adjectives usually come right before the words that they describe; however, sometimes they come after linking verbs. The articles *a, an,* and *the* are always adjectives.

Look at the following sentences that contain adjectives:

Adjectives before nouns:	*High* waves make *happy* surfers.
Adjectives after linking verbs:	The waves are *high.* The surfers are *happy.*

PRACTICE SET 1–4

Directions: Underline all the adjectives in the following sentences.

Example: <u>Several</u> people made <u>low</u> scores.

1. A gray dolphin swam beside the small boat.

2. The three passengers seemed upset.

3. The careful driver steered the car along the narrow road.

4. Nobody moved a single muscle.

5. Soon the nervous tourists left the dangerous shark in the murky water.

Adverbs

Adverbs are words that describe verbs, adjectives, or other adverbs. When trying to find adverbs, look for words that tell how, when, or where. Remember that many adverbs end in *-ly*.

Look at the following sentences that contain adverbs:

Adverb telling how: Marcus walked *carefully* along the narrow ledge.

Adverbs telling when: He *always* takes risks. He walks the ledge *daily*.

Adverb telling where: I will not walk *there*.

PRACTICE SET 1–5

Directions: Underline all the adverbs in the following sentences. On the blank, write whether the adverb tells how, when, or where.

Example: The phone rang <u>loudly</u>.   *how* _____

1. Tomorrow the teacher is giving the test. _____

2. The students must leave school early. _____

3. I will live there. _____

4. You should dress quickly. _____

5. Marshall sang well in the talent show. _____

Prepositions

Prepositions are words that connect a noun or a pronoun to the rest of the sentence. Prepositions include words like *in, on, around, under, during, of, to,* and *with*. A **prepositional phrase** starts with a preposition and ends with a noun or a pronoun.

Look at the following sentences that contain prepositional phrases:

A vase *of flowers* fell *on the floor.*

During my break, I went *to the snack bar.*

A car *with a flat tire* came *around the corner.*

PRACTICE SET 1–6

Directions: Place parentheses ( ) around all of the prepositional phrases in the following sentences. Underline the prepositions.

Example: I stood (<u>with</u> the graduates) (<u>for</u> two hours).

1. The dog with muddy paws is sleeping on the couch.

2. After dinner, we will go to the mall.

3. The letter with my signature is in the mail.

4. Several of his creations are on display.

5. Behind that bush is a nest of wasps.

Conjunctions

Conjunctions are words that join two or more words, groups of words, or sentences. Conjunctions that join equal sentences or equal parts of sentences are **coordinating conjunctions.** They are *and, but, or, nor, for, yet,* and *so.*
    Look at the following sentences that contain coordinating conjunctions:

Coordinating conjunction joining two nouns: Salt *and* pepper are popular spices.

Coordinating conjunction joining two verbs: You may bring *or* buy your lunch.

Coordinating conjunction joining two sentences: Simon will come early, *but* Miriam will be late.

Subordinating conjunctions join parts of sentences that are <u>not</u> equal. These include words like *after, although, because, before, if, since, until,* and *where.*
    Look at the following sentences that contain subordinating conjunctions:

If I get a new job, I will be able to pay my bills.

Sandra chose the used car *because* it came with a service contract.

The family likes to travel *where* they can snow-ski.

PRACTICE SET 1–7

Directions: Underline the conjunctions in the following sentences. On the blank, write whether they are coordinating or subordinating.

Example: I will stop on the way home,   *coordinating*
         or I will run out of gas.
         ___

1. If you are going to be late, call me on my   _____
   cell phone.

2. Have you seen my car keys and my wallet?   _____

3. The storm is severe, but it will miss our city.   _____

4. The car stalled because it was out of gas.   _____

5. The scary part is over, so you can open   _____
   your eyes.

Interjections

Interjections show strong feeling or emotion.
   Look at the following sentence that contains an interjection:

   Wow! You got the job!

Parts of Sentences

Do you remember the football game? Now that you have met the players and learned their names, you are ready to see what some of them will do in the actual game. Football team members play different positions, depending on the particular play. In grammar, the play is called a sentence, and the parts of speech serve different functions, depending on the nature of a particular sentence. You are now ready to see how parts of speech become parts of sentences.

Verbs

The **verb** is the most important part of the play. It creates the action or condition of the sentence. All the other parts depend on it. Look at the following examples. Notice how the sentences do not make sense without the verb.

With a verb: Her cell phone *buzzed* during a quiet moment in the concert.

Without a verb: Her cell phone during a quiet moment in the concert.

With a verb: She quickly *grabbed* her purse and *raced* to the exit door.

Without a verb: She quickly her purse and to the exit door.

PRACTICE SET 1–8

Directions: In the following sentences, underline the verbs twice.

Example: Judith finished her wedding dress.

1. Sherman's interview lasted three hours.

2. Swimming is good exercise.

3. Carla felt bad when the concert ended early.

4. I carefully printed the fliers for the trip.

5. Damien usually arrives early.

Subjects

Subjects are like quarterbacks. They make the play work. They are nouns or pronouns that cause the action or state of being to happen. They answer the question *who or what?* before the verb. Look at the subjects in the following sentences:

Common noun as subject:	The *waitress* served ten tables.
Proper noun as subject:	*Marty Brink* served ten tables.
Personal pronoun as subject:	*She* served ten tables.
Indefinite pronoun as subject:	*Somebody* served ten tables.

Notice that all the subjects tell *who* served.

PRACTICE SET 1–9

Directions: Underline the subjects of the following sentences. On the blank, write whether the subject is a noun or pronoun.

Example: Each came to the seminar   *pronoun*
with creative ideas.

1. The circus is coming to town.   _____

2. Everyone debated the issue.   _____

3. They may never ride a camel again.   _____

4. Mr. McCurdy takes the train to work.   _____

5. Some may have to pay a late fee.   _____

You have learned the basic players in English grammar. You have also learned how some of these players perform in a sentence. You are now ready to move on to the next step: understanding the plays.

TEST YOURSELF

Directions: Underline the subject once and the verb twice in each of the following sentences. Then above each word in the sentences, write its part of speech. Check your answers in the back of the book.

Example:
<u>Someone</u> <u>sat</u> in the wrong reserved seat.
(pronoun, v, prep, adj, adj, adj, n)

1. He strongly objected to the idea.

2. A neighbor raked the yard after the storm.

3. Mrs. Stanton often thought of a visit to Germany.

4. Anyone may come to the party for the mayor.

5. All persons must obey the law.

6. A friendship evolved over time.

7. The first speaker on the program was she.

8. Mushrooms grow mostly in dark caves.

9. Fishermen and sailors know the sea currents.

10. Mort goes through a precise ritual every morning.

Chapter 2

Sentence Patterns

Think about the different types of possibilities involved in a football play. When the center hikes the ball to the quarterback, the quarterback passes it to a receiver, hands it off, or perhaps keeps the ball himself and runs with it. Those who really understand football, however, know that only a limited number of patterns are possible in the game. English sentences use a limited number of patterns as well. You will learn the five basic English sentence patterns. The first type is the Subject/Verb pattern.

Sentence Pattern 1: Subject/Verb

The basic Subject/Verb sentence pattern consists of a subject and a verb. Below is a sentence in this pattern:

Fido barks.

First find the verb. The part of the sentence that includes the verb is called the **predicate.** To find the verb, ask yourself, "What happens?" Find the word that shows action or being. In the sentence above, the action is *barks,* so *barks* is the verb. The **simple subject** is the word that acts or causes the action. To find the simple subject, ask yourself, "Who barks?" The simple subject is *Fido,* the word that answers this question.

Here are some more examples in the Subject/Verb pattern:

    S   V
Anthony left early.

             S   V
The ancient *plumbing leaked* badly.

          S   V
The noisy *frog* in the pond *croaked* into the night.

PRACTICE SET 2–1

Directions: In the following sentences, underline the simple subjects once and the verbs twice.

Example: Florence <u>sat</u> on the couch.

1. The mummy returns.

2. Cool breezes blow.

3. The bacon sizzled in the hot skillet.

4. After a difficult victory, we celebrated with the team.

5. During a quiet part of the wedding ceremony, somebody sneezed noisily.

Diagramming Subject/Verb Sentence Patterns

Remember the football plays? When the coach wants to visualize the play, he draws a picture, or a diagram, of the play. He might use X's and O's to represent the opposing players and draw arrows to show the direction each player will run. Likewise, visualizing sentences is helpful in understanding the structure of English. Linguists have devised a system of diagrams to illustrate the patterns of a sentence. **Diagramming** a sentence involves placing words in a sentence on lines that connect to form a frame that shows how all of the words of the sentence are related.

The diagram for a Subject/Verb pattern looks like this:

subject	**verb**

In the sentence *Fido barks*, you already know that *barks* is the verb. To determine the subject, ask, "Who or what barks?" The answer is Fido. The simple subject is *Fido*, so *Fido* goes in the subject part of the diagram. Note that all capitalized words in the sentence are also capitalized on the diagram frame.

Fido	**barks**

Optional Practice

PRACTICE SET 2–2

Directions: Place the simple subject and verb in their appropriate places on the diagram frames. Draw the diagrams on a separate sheet of paper.

Example: Lindsay left before the finale.   Lindsay | left

1. Hector sneezed.

2. The fire blazed.

3. The old swimming hole freezes in the winter.

4. After the game, the girls celebrated.

5. In the middle of the sixth inning, the pitcher balked.

PRACTICE SET 2–3

Directions: On a separate sheet of paper, write five sentences in the Subject/Verb pattern. Then place the subjects and verbs in their appropriate positions on the diagram frame.

Sentence Pattern 2: Subject/Verb/Direct Object

Some verbs require a direct object, which is a noun or pronoun that receives the action of the verb. Examine this sentence:

John drove the car.

Begin by finding the verb. What happened? Somebody *drove*. To find the subject, ask who or what did the action. Who drove the car? John did, so *John* is the subject. To find a direct object, ask *whom or what?* after the verb. John drove (whom or) what? He drove the car, so *car* is the direct object. Thus, the subject does the action, and the **direct object** receives the action.

Here are more examples in the Subject/Verb/Direct Object pattern:

     S   V   DO
The *Red Sox won* the *game.*

     S   V   DO
LeeAnn asked Marc to the prom.

Quick Tip

Verbs that take direct objects are called **transitive verbs.** Verbs that do not take direct objects are called **intransitive verbs.** To determine whether a verb is transitive, remember to ask *whom or what?* after it, not *how?* or *when?*

I ate the sandwich.

I ate what? I ate the sandwich. In this sentence, *ate* is a transitive verb.

I ate quickly.

Does *quickly* tell whom or what? No, it tells how. In this sentence, *ate* is an intransitive verb.

PRACTICE SET 2–4

Directions: In the sentences below, underline the simple subject once and the verb twice. Write "DO" above the direct object.

Example: Rafael found his jacket.
DO

1. The farmer plowed the overgrown field.

2. The building has several floors.

3. Ray cashed his paycheck yesterday.

4. Ambition often creates conflict.

5. The Carrollwood Cardinals won the trophy.

PRACTICE SET 2–5

Directions: In the sentences below, identify the pronouns and indicate whether they are being used as subjects or direct objects.

Examples:

She left the hat in the car.   *She—subject*

Everyone kissed her on the forehead.   *Everyone—subject*

her—direct object

1. They sent him away.

2. Each received a new computer.

3. Some found the answer quickly.

4. Everything upsets him.

5. We excused them early.

Diagramming Subject/Verb/Direct Object Sentence Patterns

The Subject/Verb/Direct Object pattern diagram looks like this:

subject | verb | direct object

Place a short vertical line after the verb and then add the direct object. Notice that the line dividing the subject and the verb crosses through the horizontal base line to separate the words belonging to the subject from the words belonging to the predicate. However, to indicate that the direct object is part of the predicate, the line separating the verb from the direct object stops at the horizontal line rather than crossing through it. Look at the following diagram for placement:

subject   verb   direct object
John | drove | car

Optional Practice

PRACTICE SET 2–6

Directions: For the sentences below, place the subjects, verbs, and direct objects in their appropriate positions on the diagram frame. Draw the diagrams on a separate sheet of paper.

Example: George ate too much candy.   *George | ate | candy*

1. Annie sang a lullaby.

2. Honesty provides its own rewards.

3. The jury made a hasty decision.

4. Sydney called Morgan.

5. Sophie happily completed the difficult assignment for her science teacher.

6. Everyone needs a friend.

7. Nobody won the lottery this week.

8. He married her during halftime.

WRITING YOUR OWN SENTENCES

Directions: Fill in the blanks below, using the cues to help you write your own sentences in the Subject/Verb/Direct Object pattern. You may add *a*, *an*, or *the* if needed.

_____ _____ _____
    noun or pronoun   verb   noun or pronoun that
                                                    completes the thought

Try another one:

_____   _____   _____
noun or pronoun   verb   noun or pronoun that
                                                                        completes the thought

Now try one on your own:

_____

PRACTICE SET 2–7

Directions: On a separate sheet of paper, write five sentences in the Subject/Verb/Direct Object pattern. Then place the subjects, verbs, and direct objects in their appropriate positions on the diagram frame.

Sentence Pattern 3: Subject/Verb/Indirect Object/Direct Object

This third pattern is similar to the Subject/Verb/Direct Object pattern but with an addition. In the Subject/Verb/Indirect Object/Direct Object pattern, you go one step beyond asking *whom or what?* after the verb. The **indirect object** answers the question *to whom or what?* or *for whom or what?* and always appears between the verb and the direct object.

Here is a sentence in the Subject/Verb/Indirect Object/Direct Object pattern:

I sent John a gift.

In this sentence, *sent* is the verb. To find the subject, ask, "Who or what sent?" The answer is *I sent*, so *I* is the subject. To find the direct object, ask, "I sent whom or what?" I sent a gift, so *gift* is the direct object. To find the indirect object, ask, "To whom did I send the gift?" I sent the gift to John, so *John* is the indirect object.

To find the indirect object, ask the following questions about the verb:

To whom?	I offered Lizzie a sandwich. = I offered (to) Lizzie a sandwich.
To what?	I mailed the electric company my check. = I mailed (to) the electric company my check.
For whom?	I baked Zachary some brownies. = I baked (for) Zachary some brownies.
For what?	The client prepared the company a report. = The client prepared (for) the company a report.

In a sentence containing an indirect object, the words *to* or *for* do not actually appear before the indirect object.

> *I sent John a gift* contains an indirect object.
> *I sent a gift to John* does not contain an indirect object.

Be careful not to confuse sentences that look alike because they contain nouns that appear to occupy the same positions. Consider these two sentences:

S V   IO   DO
I sent Marcy some flowers.

S V   DO
I sent Marcy to the store.

In the first sentence, *flowers* is the direct object, telling what I sent. I sent what? *Flowers. Marcy* is the indirect object: I sent (to) *Marcy* some flowers. In the second sentence, *Marcy* is the direct object. Whom did I send? I sent *Marcy. To the store* is a phrase telling where I sent her. This sentence does not contain an indirect object.

Try another example.

Glenna painted her teacher a picture.

Painted is the verb. Who or what painted? Glenna did, so *Glenna* is the subject. Remember to ask the appropriate questions to distinguish the direct object from the indirect object. To determine the indirect object, ask *for whom* Glenna painted. Glenna painted *for* her teacher, so *teacher* is the indirect object. To determine the direct object, ask, "*What* did Glenna paint?" Glenna painted (for her teacher) the picture, so *picture* is the direct object.

Here are some other examples in the Subject/Verb/Indirect Object/Direct Object pattern:

S   V   IO   DO
Dorothy offered Melanie an *explanation.*

S   V   IO   DO
The *actors gave* the *audience* a *hand.*

S   V   IO   DO
Marisol sent her *friend* a *letter* written in Portuguese.

Like subjects and direct objects, indirect objects are nouns or words that function as nouns.

N   N   N
Winston taught Denny a song.

In addition, certain verbs, such as *ask, bring, buy, give, send, show, teach,* and *tell,* often have indirect objects.

It is not possible to have an indirect object in a sentence that does not have a direct object. For example, look at the sentence *Glenna painted her teacher a picture*. If the direct object (*a picture*) is deleted, the sentence says, *Glenna painted her teacher*.

PRACTICE SET 2–8

Directions: In the following sentences, underline the simple subjects once and the verbs twice. Then label the indirect objects (IO) and direct objects (DO). Not all sentences contain direct objects or indirect objects.

1. Dora sat calmly by the window during the thunderstorm.

2. Michelle taught her brother a lesson about manners.

3. Kyle gave Madison the wrong directions to his house.

4. They smuggled cans of soda into the stadium.

5. Chris showed his friends his new MP3 player.

6. I give anyone in social work much respect.

7. Ellie kept the stray puppy in her garage.

8. Rob went to dinner with his girlfriend.

9. Morgan teaches dolphins sign language.

10. Amy baked Steve an apple pie.

Diagramming Subject/Verb/Indirect Object/Direct Object Sentence Patterns

To diagram Subject/Verb/Indirect Object/Direct Object sentence patterns, begin with the parts you already know. For example, in the sentence *Glenna painted her teacher a picture*, you have already determined that *Glenna* is the subject, *painted* is the verb, and *picture* is the direct object:

$$\text{Glenna} \mid \text{painted} \mid \text{picture}$$

Place the indirect object on a horizontal line (_____) attached to a back-slash diagonal, which extends slightly below the horizontal line.

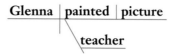

PRACTICE SET 2–9

Directions: For the sentences below, place the subjects, verbs, indirect objects, and direct objects in their appropriate positions on the diagram frame. Draw the diagrams on a separate sheet of paper.

Example: The teacher gave the entire class a lecture.

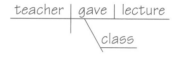

1. The supervisor asked Meredith some difficult questions.

2. The con man sold Carolyn some land in the Cypress Swamp.

3. Terri fed her iguanas a beautiful salad.

4. Dr. Totten sent the laboratory a detailed report.

5. Madonna sang the audience another encore.

6. She brought him a pineapple pizza for lunch.

7. Valerie presented him an ultimatum.

8. The job offered her a chance to travel.

WRITING YOUR OWN SENTENCES

Directions: Fill in the blanks below, using the cues to help you write your own sentences in the Subject/Verb/Indirect Object/Direct Object pattern. You may add *a*, *an*, or *the* if needed.

_____	_____	_____	_____
noun or pronoun	choose one of the following verbs: *ask, bring, buy, give, send, show, teach, tell*	noun or pronoun	noun or pronoun that completes the thought

Try another one:

noun or pronoun	choose one of the following verbs: *ask, bring, buy, give, send, show, teach, tell*	noun or pronoun	noun or pronoun that completes the thought

Now try one on your own:

PRACTICE SET 2–10

Directions: On a separate sheet of paper, construct five of your own sentences in the Subject/Verb/Indirect Object/Direct Object pattern. Then place just the subjects, verbs, indirect objects, and direct objects in the appropriate positions on the diagram frame.

Sentence Pattern 4: Subject/Verb/Direct Object/Object Complement

This pattern contains the subject, verb, and direct object, but it adds another word, the object complement. An **object complement** always follows the direct object and either describes or renames the direct object. Consider this sentence:

She named the baby Bruce.

The verb is *named*. To find the subject, ask, "Who or what named?" The answer is *she* named, so *she* is the subject. Now ask, "Whom or what did she name?" She named the baby, so *baby* is the direct object. Any word following the direct object that renames or describes the direct object is an object complement. She named the baby Bruce, so *Bruce* is the object complement.

Quick Tip

Object complements can be nouns, pronouns, or adjectives. When an adjective functions as the object complement, it describes the direct object before it rather than renaming it:

I painted my nails *green*.

Painted is the verb. Who or what painted? I did, so *I* is the subject. What did I paint? I painted my nails, so *nails* is the direct object. What did I paint them? I painted them green, so *green* is the object complement, describing nails.

In addition, certain verbs, such as *appoint, believe, call, choose, consider, elect, keep, leave, make, name, paint, prove, select, think, turn,* and *vote,* commonly appear in patterns with object complements.

Here is another sentence in the Subject/Verb/Direct Object/Object Complement pattern. To find the direct object, remember to ask *whom or what?* about the verb. To find the object complement, remember to ask *what?* about the direct object.

what what

S   V   DO OC

The *dye turned* the *shirt red.*

Look at some more examples in this pattern:

S   V   DO   OC (noun)

The *panel selected Dong Li Miss Universe.*

S   V   DO   OC (adjective)

The *doctor considered* the patient's *feelings important.*

S   V   DO   OC (adjective)

The *party* at the amusement park *made* the little girl's *friends happy.*

Be careful not to confuse sentences that look alike. Consider these two sentences:

He called the man a liar.

He called the man yesterday.

Man is the direct object in both sentences. In the first sentence, *liar* renames the man, so it is the object complement. In the second sentence, *yesterday* simply tells when he called the man. This sentence does not contain an object complement.

PRACTICE SET 2–11

Directions: In the following sentences, underline the simple subjects once and the verbs twice. Then label the direct objects (DO) and object complements (OC).

DO   OC

Example: We named our boat *Hog Heaven.*

1. He called his brother a sissy.

2. The dye turned my hair purple.

3. I proved him wrong today.

4. The comedian left the audience hungry for more.

5. I kept Nicky busy during the boring speech.

6. The committee appointed me the leader.

7. Carlie made me sorry about my behavior.

8. I consider you my friend.

Diagramming Subject/Verb/Direct Object/Object Complement Sentence Patterns

To diagram a sentence in the Subject/Verb/Direct Object/Object Complement pattern, begin with the parts you already know.

$$\text{subject} \mid \text{verb} \mid \text{direct object}$$

The object complement follows a backslash placed next to the direct object. Notice how the line points back to the direct object, the word the object complement renames or describes.

$$\text{subject} \mid \text{verb} \mid \text{direct object} \setminus \text{object complement}$$

$$\text{I} \mid \text{painted} \mid \text{nails} \setminus \text{green}$$

Optional Practice

PRACTICE SET 2–12

Directions: For the sentences below, place the subjects, verbs, direct objects, and object complements in their appropriate positions on the diagram frame. Draw the diagrams on a separate sheet of paper.

Example: We elected Jack secretary.   We | elected | Jack \ secretary

1. *American Idol* made Simon Cowell a celebrity.

2. Joey's sarcastic comment left Belinda speechless.

3. Joe Torre called the New York Yankees unbeatable.

4. I consider Dr. Dayan an expert.

5. The boss appointed his new secretary chairperson of the United Way campaign.

WRITING YOUR OWN SENTENCES

Directions: Fill in the blanks below, using the cues to help you write your own sentences in the Subject/Verb/Direct Object/Object Complement pattern. You may add *a*, *an*, or *the* if needed.

noun or pronoun	one of the following verbs: *appoint, believe, call, choose, consider, elect, keep, leave, make, name, paint, prove, select, think, turn, vote*	noun or pronoun	noun, pronoun, or adjective that renames or describes the noun or pronoun just before it

Try another one:

noun or pronoun	one of the following verbs: *appoint, believe, call, choose, consider, elect, keep, leave, make, name, paint, prove, select, think, turn, vote*	noun or pronoun	noun, pronoun, or adjective that renames or describes the noun or pronoun just before it

Now try one on your own:

PRACTICE SET 2–13

Directions: On a separate sheet of paper, write five sentences in the Subject/Verb/ Direct Object/Object Complement pattern. Then place the subjects, verbs, direct objects, and object complements in their appropriate positions on the diagram frame.

Sentence Pattern 5: Subject/Linking Verb/Subject Complement

The verbs examined so far have been action verbs. You have learned that some action verbs are **intransitive verbs,** that is, verbs that do not take a direct object. Remember Fido? Fido *barks.* Other action verbs are **transitive verbs,** which do take a direct object. Remember John and his car? John drove the car, so *car* is the direct object.

Not all verbs show action, however. **Linking verbs** have a special purpose—to link another word to the subject in order to explain or enhance the subject's meaning.

> Lindsay seems lucky.

In this sentence, *lucky* tells something about the subject, *Lindsay.* The verb *seems* links the word *lucky* to *Lindsay.* Verbs such as *seem, appear,* and *become* are usually

Quick Tip

A good trick to determine if a verb is a linking verb is to substitute the word *seems* for the verb. If the sentence still makes sense, the verb is a linking verb.

> The food *looked* spoiled.
> The food *seemed* spoiled.

Seemed works, so *looked* is a linking verb in the sentence above.

> I *looked* at the dark clouds.
> I *seemed* at the dark clouds.

Seemed doesn't work, so *looked* is not a linking verb in the sentence above.

linking verbs. Other verbs can also be linking verbs, such as those involving the senses, including *feel, sound, taste, smell,* and *look.* These verbs are linking verbs only when they connect the subject to a word that renames or describes it. Be careful not to consider them linking verbs when they show action. Examine these two sentences:

Hilda tastes the chocolate.

The chocolate tastes bitter.

In the first sentence, Hilda is doing something. She tastes the chocolate. Here *tastes* shows action. In the second sentence, *tastes* connects *bitter* to the word it describes—*chocolate.* In this sentence, it is a linking verb.

PRACTICE SET 2–14

Directions: For the sentences below, underline the verbs twice and then determine whether the verbs are linking verbs or action verbs.

Examples:

He <u>looked</u> at the webpage carefully.   *action*

He <u>looked</u> confused.   *linking*

1. Jason suddenly appeared in the window.   _____

2. The track star's running shoes smelled terrible.   _____

3. I felt the rough surface of the tabletop.   _____

4. She sounded the bell at midnight.   _____

5. The Tin Man appeared rusty.   _____

6. I really feel sorry for you.   _____

7. The campers smelled the skunk in the woods.   _____

8. His excuse sounds insincere to me.   _____

9. The climber became weary near the summit.   _____

10. His prospects looked grim.   _____

Another important linking verb is the verb *to be.* In fact, the forms of the verb *to be* are the most common linking verbs.

Albert *is* an actor.

Jessica *was* fortunate.

Any form of the verb *to be* can be a linking verb: *am, is, are, was, were.* Be, been, and *being* can also be linking verbs when they appear with helping verbs (*will be, has been, are being*).

Like the verbs of the senses, forms of *to be* are not always linking verbs. Sometimes they are **auxiliary verbs,** that is, verbs that combine with other verbs to form a verb phrase:

> verb phrase
> I *am running.*

> verb phrase
> You *were snoring.*

You will learn more about verb phrases in Chapter 4.

PRACTICE SET 2–15

Directions: In the sentences below, underline the linking verbs twice.

Example: He was hungry all week.

1. They are sailors in the United States Navy.

2. Martine is sorry about her mistake.

3. I am certain that Darcy left.

4. My sister was happy when I called her.

5. The twins are ushers at that movie theater.

6. You are silly.

7. Michael and Thomas were friends in kindergarten.

8. I am careful about what I say.

You can now recognize three types of linking verbs:

Verbs such as *seem, become, appear*

Verbs dealing with the senses, such as *feel, smell, taste, look, sound*

Forms of *to be,* such as *am, is, are, was, were, be, been, being*

When the verb in the sentence is a linking verb, the word that it links to the subject is called the subject complement. A **subject complement** is a word that follows a linking verb and renames or describes the subject. Subject complements can be nouns, pronouns, or adjectives:

> S   LV   SC (noun)
> Shelly is a *student* of history.

Don't confuse subject complements with direct objects. Like direct objects, subject complements answer the question *who or what?* about the verb. *Amelia Earhart was a pilot.* She was a what? A pilot. However, *pilot* is a subject complement, not a direct object, because it follows the linking verb *was. Pilot* does not receive the action of the verb but, instead, renames the subject, *Amelia Earhart.*

       S   LV   SC (noun)
Jack became a tour *director* in Europe.

       S LV SC (adjective)
She was *alone* for three years.

         S   LV   SC (adjective)
The sky appeared *black* before the storm.

Here are more sentences in the Subject/Linking Verb/Subject Complement pattern:

        S   LV SC (adjective)
Marianne looked healthy.

        S   LV   SC (noun)
Mr. Martinelli is a large *man.*

Don't assume that all *to be* verbs are either linking verbs or part of a verb phrase. A *to be* verb can also come before a word designating time or place:

    The game was yesterday.
    My doctor is away.

Words that designate time or place are adverbs. You will learn more about them in Chapter 3.

Diagramming Subject/Linking Verb/ Subject Complement Sentence Patterns

The Subject/Verb/Subject Complement diagram frame is similar to the Subject/ Verb/Direct Object diagram frame. The only difference is that the line between the verb and the subject complement slants to the left, pointing back to the subject renamed or described.

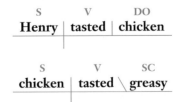

PRACTICE SET 2–16

Directions: For the sentences below, place the subjects, verbs, and subject complements in their appropriate positions on the diagram frame. Draw the diagrams on a separate sheet of paper.

Example: The windows were foggy. ̲w̲i̲n̲d̲o̲w̲s̲ | were \ foggy

1. The trophy was enormous.

2. Wynton Marsalis is a trumpeter.

3. The tacos looked spicy.

4. The winner was he.

5. My answer sounded stupid.

6. The cold seemed unbearable.

7. My uncles were fishermen.

8. Tallahassee is the capital of Florida.

WRITING YOUR OWN SENTENCES

Directions: Fill in the blanks below, using the cues to help you write your own sentences in the Subject/Linking Verb/Subject Complement pattern.

| noun or pronoun | linking verb, like *be, seem, become, appear,* verb of the senses | noun, pronoun, or adjective linking to the subject |

Try another one:

| noun or pronoun | linking verb, like *be, seem, become, appear,* verb of the senses | noun, pronoun, or adjective linking to the subject |

Now try one on your own:

_____

PRACTICE SET 2–17

Directions: On a separate sheet of paper, write five sentences in the Subject/Linking Verb/Subject Complement pattern. Then place the subjects, linking verbs, and subject complements in their appropriate positions on the diagram frame.

TEST YOURSELF

Directions: Identify the sentence patterns of the following sentences and write the pattern on the lines provided.

Example: Kevin asked a silly question.   _S/V/DO_

1. Arthur sold Ricky his old car.   _____

2. Bert is a very smart guy.   _____

3. Katherine won first prize at the fair.   _____

4. Elena considered her son brilliant.   _____

5. Mashid left his keys in his locked car.   _____

6. Our hot water heater broke last week.   _____

7. Mazie colored the tree orange.   _____

8. The speaker told the crowd the story of his life.   _____

9. They were all good dancers.   _____

10. The final exam was very easy.   _____

WORD WATCHERS

Some words sound alike but have very different meanings. Be sure to use the words that you mean.

accept/except   *Accept* is a verb meaning *to receive:*   I accept your apology.

Except is a preposition meaning *but:*   Everyone was invited except Tim.

(continued)

WORD WATCHERS *(cont.)*

affect/effect   Both can mean *influence. Affect* is a verb: How does the weather affect your mood?
Effect is a noun: The weather has no effect on my mood.

Effect can also be a verb meaning *to bring about:*   I want to effect a change in policy.

between/among   Use *between* for two; use *among* for more than two: I divided the chores between the twins but among the triplets.

capital/capitol   The *capital* is a city; the *capitol* is a building: The capital of Florida is Tallahassee; many state capitols have copper domes.

choose/chose   *Choose*, rhyming with *fuse*, means to select: Please choose your partner.

Its past tense is *chose*, rhyming with *hose:*   He chose the same partner last week.

WORD WATCHERS PRACTICE SET

Directions: Choose the correct word in the parentheses.

1. How does this grade (affect/effect) my overall grade point average?

2. Mr. Callahan spread the workload (between/among) all of the students in the class.

3. The (capital/capitol) of Vermont is Montpelier.

4. Tie a ribbon on every chair (accept/except) that one.

5. Lilly (choose/chose) the low-calorie dessert.

6. The senator gave his speech on the steps of the (capital/capitol) building.

7. You must (accept/except) responsibility for your actions.

8. The nuclear reactor accident had a devastating (affect/effect) on the village.

9. You can (choose/chose) the path you wish to take in life.

10. Please place your luggage (between/among) the two posts.

Chapter 3

Adjectives and Adverbs

Adjectives

Although there are many kinds of adjectives, the following two rules apply to all of them:

1. Adjectives **modify** (describe**) nouns** and **pronouns.**

2. Adjectives tell **which one, what kind,** and **how many.**

An adjective usually appears before the noun it modifies. Examine this sentence:

I love my *new* car.

What word does *new* describe? It describes the noun *car*. Thus, you know that *new* is an adjective because it describes a noun. It tells *which* car or *what kind of* car—my *new* car. Since adjectives tell which one or what kind, *new* is an adjective.

Articles

English has two indefinite articles, *a* and *an*, and one definite article, *the*. Since articles modify nouns and pronouns, they are adjectives. Articles are like signposts on a highway. They show that a noun is coming, though it may not be the very next word. For this reason, they are noun indicators.

The rusty hinge broke.

This sentence contains a noun indicator, the article *the;* however, it does not directly precede the noun it indicates.

Possessives

A **possessive** shows ownership. Possessive words are adjectives when they modify nouns and pronouns.

I love *Angie's* car.

What word does *Angie's* describe? It describes *car*. Because *car* is a noun, the word *Angie's* must be an adjective. The adjective *Angie's* tells which car. Possessives also imply indirect ownership: *today's news, society's values*.

Like possessive nouns, possessive adjectives (*my, your, his, her, its, our,* and *their*) modify nouns and function as adjectives.

> *My* leg is broken.   They offered *their* apology.

Most authorities list all of the possessives as personal pronouns. When analyzing possessives in a sentence, however, you should distinguish between possessive pronouns and possessive adjectives. Possessive pronouns (*mine, yours, his, hers, its, ours, theirs*) take the place of nouns.

Pronoun: *Yours* is on the bottom.

Possessive adjectives (*my, your, his, her, its, our, their*) modify nouns.

Adjective: *Your* test is on the bottom.

Predicate Adjectives

Adjectives don't always appear next to the word they modify. Look at this sentence:

> My car was *new*.

New describes the noun *car*. It tells what kind of car—a *new* car. This sentence follows the Subject/Verb/Subject Complement sentence pattern.

Car is the subject, and *was* is a linking verb. What is the function of the word *new*? Since it follows a linking verb, it is a subject complement. Subject complements can be only three parts of speech—nouns, pronouns, or adjectives. In this sentence, *new* describes *car*, so it is an adjective. When adjectives serve as subject complements, they always appear in the predicate of the sentence. For this reason, they are called predicate adjectives. **Predicate adjectives** follow linking verbs and modify the subject; thus, *new* is a predicate adjective.

PRACTICE SET 3–1

Directions: Circle the adjectives in the following sentences and underline the words they modify. Above the underlined word, write its part of speech.

> Example: I took (your) (CD) player to (the) (main) office.
>   noun   noun

1. I found the ancient relic in a dark cave.

2. The hit movie of last summer was a computer-generated cartoon.

3. I always stop on long trips to view scenic bridges.

4. My youngest daughter likes to eat sour pickles and hot peppers.

5. Sydney's ankle turned a bright purple after her unfortunate accident.

6. The possibilities are endless.

7. I took piano lessons after second grade.

8. Lynda's grandmother was a fabulous cook.

9. The unfortunate musician broke a violin string during the concerto.

10. His biography is the untold story of a heroic farm boy.

Parts of Speech

Adjectives have many technical names.

Proper Adjectives

Proper adjectives refer to particular persons, places, or things and begin with a capital letter.

> This *Renaissance* painting is very valuable.

Demonstrative Adjectives

When *this, that, these,* and *those* modify nouns, they are demonstrative adjectives.

> *This* meat is raw.

Indefinite Adjectives

When the indefinite pronouns *each, every, either, neither, another, all, some, many, most,* and *both* modify nouns, they become indefinite adjectives.

> *Every* child deserves a good home.

Interrogative Adjectives

When the interrogative pronouns *what, which,* and *whose* modify nouns, they become interrogative adjectives.

> *Which* answer is correct?

Relative Adjectives

When *what, whatever, which, whichever,* and *whose* modify nouns, they become relative adjectives.

> *Whatever* answer I choose will be correct.

(continued)

Parts of Speech
(cont.)

Numerical Adjectives

When cardinal numbers (the whole numbers, like *one, two, three*) or ordinal numbers (the numbers that show position, like *first, second, third*) modify nouns, they become numerical adjectives.

Two people offered to help me.   My *first* reason is simple.

PRACTICE SET 3–2

Directions: Circle the adjectives in the following sentences and underline the words they modify. Above each underlined word, write its part of speech.

Example: (Three) graduates filled (these) positions.

1. He is the last customer in line.

2. What choice do I have?

3. Each time you sneezed, he laughed.

4. I like whatever meal you serve.

5. Lisa's answer made me smile.

6. Seventy-six trombones led the big parade.

7. Which position do you play?

8. I know whose fault it is.

9. You are the second person to ask me that question.

10. The Australian actor won the Oscar.

Adding Adjectives to the Diagram

Adjectives have two positions on the diagram frame. Predicate adjectives, the adjectives that follow linking verbs and serve as subject complements, appear on the main line, following the linking verb and a backslash diagonal line:

He | is \ happy

All other adjectives go on a backslash diagonal line beneath the word they modify. If more than one adjective modifies the same word, each has its own diagonal. Do not place an adjective directly under a verb since adjectives never modify verbs.

The strong, healthy athlete exercised.

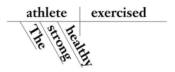

The poor, lonesome beggar gave the wealthy man his last dime.

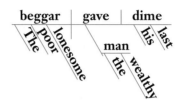

PRACTICE SET 3–3

Directions: Diagram the following sentences, placing the adjectives in the appropriate positions.

Example: My current boyfriend has four sisters.

1. I met an old Russian woman.

2. Several English courses are available.

3. Three strange sea creatures occupied the aquarium.

4. Karen's math teacher gave the confused student some additional notes.

5. That requirement seems unnecessary.

6. Mrs. Spear sold the expensive house.

7. The contest judges gave each contestant a cheap plastic medal.

8. Which sandwich tastes fresh?

9. Dr. Patel is an American citizen.

10. The handsome prince sent the beautiful princess a fragrant rose.

Adverbs

Two rules apply to all adverbs:

1. Adverbs modify **verbs, adjectives,** and other **adverbs.**

   An adverb modifying a verb: She **sang** *beautifully.* (describes how she **sang**)

   An adverb modifying an adjective: He is *very* **sorry.** (describes how **sorry** he is)

   An adverb modifying another adverb: He walked *quite* **slowly.** (describes how **slowly**)

2. Adverbs tell **where, when, how, why,** and **to what degree.**

An adverb telling where:	She placed the paper *there*.
An adverb telling when:	He *never* lies to me.
An adverb telling how:	She spoke *angrily*.
An adverb telling to what degree:	He is *not* happy.

Adverbs that tell why usually appear as phrases or clauses: I am angry *because she is late.*

Adverbs Ending in -ly

Adverbs often end in *-ly*. When modifiers have two forms, one with the *-ly* ending and one without, distinguishing the adverb from the adjective is easy. For example, *real* is an adjective and *really* is an adverb. However, some words that are not adverbs end in *-ly*. Consider this example:

She is a lovely girl.

Although *lovely* ends in *-ly*, it modifies a noun, *girl*. Thus, it is an adjective, not an adverb. Rather than simply noting the *-ly* ending, ask yourself what the word tells and what part of speech the word modifies.

Interrogative Adverbs

The interrogative words *how*, *when*, *why*, and *where* are adverbs. We use these adverbs to ask questions.

Why did you do that?   *Where* is my hat?

PRACTICE SET 3–4

Directions: Label the adjectives (adj.) and adverbs (adv.) in the following sentences, and draw an arrow to the words they modify.

Example: The long movie ended sadly.

1. The child cried very loudly.

2. Yesterday, the only plane arrived too late.

3. The rather sad story depressed me.

4. He took the fairly difficult exam quickly.

5. Arabella plays the piano extremely well.

6. Mitzi quite happily addressed the crowd.

7. I carefully dyed the ugly dress bright blue.

8. I never gave Frank that letter.

9. You seem so unhappy tonight.

10. I definitely left the contract there.

Adding Adverbs to the Diagram

Use a backslash diagonal to place the adverb beneath the word it modifies. If the adverb modifies another word (an adjective or another adverb) that is already written on a backslash diagonal, add a short connecting line to the first backslash before creating a new one.

Rick left quickly.   He sang very badly.

```
  Rick  |  left            He   |  sang
        \                        \
         \quickly                 \badly
                                   \very
```

PRACTICE SET 3–5

Directions: Diagram the following sentences containing adjectives and adverbs.

Example: Iris found a diamond ring yesterday.

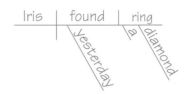

1. The lazy dog slept.

2. Daniel laughed hysterically.

3. My only brother is just thirteen.

4. Each father proudly gave his son a merit badge.

5. Robert's wife is a lawyer.

6. Those incredibly ancient ruins attract many tourists yearly.

7. He is never late.

8. I always call my mother "Mama."

9. The finicky eater gave the exasperated waiter a new order.

10. That very sensitive information became public yesterday.

11. Your lame excuse is definitely not acceptable.

12. His fiftieth birthday party was really fun.

TEST YOURSELF

Directions: Label all of the adjectives and adverbs in the following sentences.

<pre>
        adj. adj.   adv.   adj. adj.   adj. adv.
Example: A Roman soldier proudly entered the crowded city after a very

        adj.
        decisive victory.
</pre>

1. Great apes live peacefully in completely protected areas.

2. His car skidded sharply into the wrong lane.

3. Mark's sister was so happy that she finally got a very high raise in her salary.

4. Yesterday, my friend found a unique stamp for her new collection.

5. The messengers quickly recognized that most people were not ready for bad news.

6. The proud winner immediately ran to the nearest telephone.

7. In modern communication, short, concise e-mails have replaced long, wordy letters.

8. We never consider the serious consequences when we make a too hasty decision.

9. One should always allow for some mistakes in a bank account.

10. The seaside community had not expected a high tide.

COMPOSITION WARM-UP

Directions: Add adjectives or adverbs to make the following sentences *more* specific.

1. Many college students have _____ problems.
adjective

2. _____ shows have always been popular on television.
adjective

3. The cost of living has increased _____.
adverb

4. Fast food restaurants offer _____ and _____ meals.
adjective   adjective

5. Exercising _____ helps senior citizens stay healthy.
adverb

6. Politicians often run _____ campaigns.
adjective

7. Owen drives more _____ than his father does.
adverb

8. Jackson plays the trumpet very _____.
adverb

9. The rescue workers felt _____ after the hurricane.
adjective

10. I _____ asked my boss for a raise.
adverb

COMPOSITION PRACTICE

Directions: Write five sentences on a topic of your choice, remembering to include colorful adjectives and adverbs to make your ideas specific.

WORD WATCHERS

Some words sound alike but have very different meanings. Be sure to use the words that you mean.

cite/site/sight	*Cite* refers to giving reference: You must cite each article you read for this research paper.
	Site refers to a place: This corner is the site of the accident.
	Sight refers to vision: John Milton lost his sight before he wrote *Paradise Lost*.
complement/compliment	Remember the vowels to keep these straight. *Comple*ment means *to complete* and the spelling is similar: Your purse really complements your outfit.
	To *compliment*—with an *i*—means to say something nice about someone: I like to get a compliment—spelled with an I. Thanks for paying me that compliment!
continuous/continual	When something is *continuous*, it goes without a break: The dog's continuous barking disturbed the entire neighborhood.
	Something that is *continual* happens regularly and frequently, but not necessarily continuously: His continual interruption angered the instructor.
emigrate/immigrate	Remember the vowels. People **e**migrate (**e**xit) FROM a country; people **i**mmigrate (go **i**nto) TO their new country: The O'Rourkes emigrated from Ireland in 1988. Thousands of people immigrate to the United States each year.
farther/further	*Farther* refers to distance: They live farther away than they used to.
	Further refers to quantity of degree: I do not wish to discuss this topic any further.

(continued)

WORD WATCHERS
(*cont.*)

WORD WATCHERS PRACTICE SET

Directions: Choose the correct word in the parentheses.

1. The (continuous/continual) dripping of the faucet kept everyone awake.

2. If you escalate this argument any (farther/further), you will lose my support.

3. We chose an unusual (cite/site) for the annual picnic.

4. The red wine (complemented/complimented) the filet mignon perfectly.

5. Before she (emigrated/immigrated) to the United States, Luisa completed her college education in Bolivia.

6. Nebraska Avenue is (farther/further) from the expressway than Kennedy Boulevard.

7. Their (continuous/continual) arguing is going to wreck their marriage.

8. The professor (cited/sited/sighted) Albert Einstein in his lecture.

9. May I (complement/compliment) you on your good manners?

10. Anatoly brought his violin with him when he (emigrated/immigrated) from Russia.

Chapter 4

Phrases

A phrase is a group of related words that does not contain both a subject and a verb. A phrase functions as a single part of speech—a noun, a verb, an adjective, or an adverb. Several types of phrases exist in English. One of the most common types of phrases begins with words called prepositions.

Prepositional Phrases

A **preposition** is a word that connects nouns and/or pronouns to other words in a sentence. A preposition is usually one word, but sometimes a group of words can act as a preposition. Below is a list of common prepositions.

about	beside	in spite of	through
above	between	inside	throughout
according to	beyond	instead of	to
across	but (meaning except)	into	together with
after	by	like	toward
against	by way of	near	under
along	concerning	of	underneath
along with	despite	off	until
among	down	on	up
around	during	onto	up to
as	except	out	upon
as well as	for	out of	with
at	from	outside	with reference to
because of	in	over	with regard to
before	in addition to	past	with the exception of
behind	in back of	regarding	within
below	in case of	since	without
beneath	in front of	than	

A **prepositional phrase** always begins with a preposition and ends with a noun or a pronoun, which is called the **object of the preposition.** Between the preposition and the object, some modifiers may appear.

prep. O
The meaning *of life* is a mystery.

prep.   O
I found my ring *among* the old *newspapers.*

To plus a **noun** = a prepositional phrase:

I went *to* **school.**

To plus a **verb** is not a prepositional phrase:

I like *to* **sing.**

This construction is an **infinitive.** See Chapter 5 for more information on infinitives.

PRACTICE SET 4–1

Directions: In the sentences below, place parentheses around all prepositional phrases, and underline the objects of the prepositions.

Example: The winner (of the game) advances (to the finals).

1. According to the police, the accident on the overpass was very serious.

2. We have not received your payment for January.

3. A person like him is always an asset to this firm.

4. He proposed to her during the football game.

5. Everyone except Felicia knows about your unusual rose garden.

6. Do not open before Christmas.

7. Just between us, I bought these shoes in spite of her objections.

8. She lied about the burglary that had taken place during their trip to Canada in March.

9. At night, my ferret sleeps among the boxes under my bed.

10. Rolando found the missing map inside the rusty watering can we had thrown in front of the storage shed.

Prepositional Phrases as Adjectives and Adverbs

Adjective Phrases

Prepositional phrases can function as adjectives. Just like one-word adjectives, prepositional phrases can describe **which one** and **what kind** about a **noun** or a **pronoun.**

> The snake *in that cage* is poisonous.

(The prepositional phrase *in that cage* tells **which** snake.)

> You should not submit a resumé *with a typographical error.*

(The prepositional phrase *with a typographical error* tells **what kind** of resumé.)

PRACTICE SET 4–2

Directions: In the sentences below, place each prepositional phrase in parentheses and write it in the blank. In the second blank, write the word that the phrase modifies.

Example: I thought the program (about the election) was very interesting.

Prepositional phrase: *about the election*

Word it modifies: *program*

1. The members of our club hope you will join us soon.

Prepositional phrase: _____

Word it modifies: _____

2. Jill told a funny story about her nosy uncle.

Prepositional phrase: _____

Word it modifies: _____

3. The famous tenor sang a song about young love.

Prepositional phrase: _____

Word it modifies: _____

4. The shop around the corner sells what you need.

Prepositional phrase: _____

Word it modifies: _____

5. I wrote him a letter concerning his recent engagement to Sophia.

Prepositional phrase: _____

Word it modifies: _____

Prepositional phrase: _____

Word it modifies: _____

Adverb Phrases

Prepositional phrases can also function as adverbs. Just like one-word adverbs, prepositional phrases can modify **verbs, adjectives,** or other **adverbs,** and they can tell **where, when, how, why,** and **to what degree** about the words they modify.

I put the report *in the file.*

(The prepositional phrase *in the file* tells **where** I put the report.)

She sold her car *on Friday.*

(The prepositional phrase *on Friday* tells **when** she sold her car.)

The baker made this cake *with a blender.*

(The prepositional phrase *with a blender* tells **how** the baker made this cake.)

Daniel bought a book *for his brother.*

(The prepositional phrase *for his brother* tells **why** Daniel bought a book.)

PRACTICE SET 4–3

Directions: In the sentences below, place each prepositional phrase in parentheses and write it in the blank. In the second blank, write the word that the phrase modifies.

Example: (Throughout the production), the actors spoke in rhyme.

Prepositional phrase: Throughout the production

Word it modifies: spoke

1. She stored the stolen letters behind the cabinet.

Prepositional phrase: _____

Word it modifies: _____

2. At dawn the sheriff found the cattle rustler.

   Prepositional phrase: _____

   Word it modifies: _____

3. I took these pictures with an old box camera.

   Prepositional phrase: _____

   Word it modifies: _____

4. Our neighbors live beyond their means.

   Prepositional phrase: _____

   Word it modifies: _____

5. We can join you for lunch after class.

   Prepositional phrase: _____

   Word it modifies: _____

   Prepositional phrase: _____

   Word it modifies: _____

PRACTICE SET 4–4

Directions: In the sentences below, place each prepositional phrase in parentheses and write it in the blank. Next, determine the word that each phrase modifies and the part of speech of the word it modifies. Then indicate whether the prepositional phrase acts as an adjective or an adverb.

Example: The parrot (in the cage) can talk.

Prepositional phrase: _in the cage_____

Word it modifies: _parrot_____

Part of speech of the word it modifies: _noun_____

Prepositional phrase functions as this
part of speech: _adjective_____

1. During the snowstorm, our heater broke.

   Prepositional phrase: _____

   Word it modifies: _____

   Part of speech of the word it modifies: _____

   Prepositional phrase functions as this
   part of speech: _____

2. The eye of the hurricane is near.

   Prepositional phrase: _____

   Word it modifies: _____

   Part of speech of the word it modifies: _____

   Prepositional phrase functions as this
   part of speech: _____

3. I find myself in a difficult position.

   Prepositional phrase: _____

   Word it modifies: _____

   Part of speech of the word it modifies: _____

   Prepositional phrase functions as this
   part of speech: _____

4. He fell into the lake.

   Prepositional phrase: _____

   Word it modifies: _____

   Part of speech of the word it modifies: _____

   Prepositional phrase functions as this
   part of speech: _____

5. The man with the broken leg needed help after the accident.

   Prepositional phrase: _____

   Word it modifies: _____

Part of speech of the word it modifies: _____

Prepositional phrase functions as this
part of speech: _____

Prepositional phrase: _____

Word it modifies: _____

Part of speech of the word it modifies: _____

Prepositional phrase functions as this
part of speech: _____

Adding Prepositional Phrases to the Diagram

The frame for the prepositional phrase is a backslash diagonal line for the preposition, extending slightly below a horizontal line for its object. Place any modifiers on backslash diagonals beneath the object.

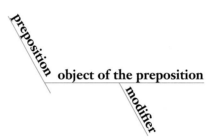

To decide where to place the prepositional phrase frame, determine whether the phrase is an adjective or an adverb. What does the phrase tell?

If the phrase tells **which one** or **what kind,** it is an **adjective** phrase.

If the phrase tells **where, when, why,** or **how,** it is an **adverb** phrase.

What part of speech does the phrase modify?

If the phrase modifies a **noun** or **pronoun,** it is an **adjective** phrase.

If the phrase modifies a **verb,** an **adjective,** or an **adverb,** it is an **adverb** phrase.

Examine this sentence:

The meaning of life is a mystery.

The diagram of the sentence looks like this:

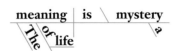

Sometimes a prepositional phrase can modify the object of a different prepositional phrase. Consider this sentence:

I put the ticket on the corner of my desk.

On the corner and *of my desk* are both prepositional phrases, but what does each modify? *On the corner* tells **where** I put the ticket. Since it tells **where** and describes a verb, it is an adverb phrase.

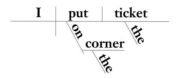

What does *of my desk* tell? It tells **which** corner. Since it tells **which one** and it describes a noun, it is an **adjective** phrase. It modifies the object of the preposition—*corner.* Diagram it like this:

What does *of my desk* tell? It tells **which** corner. Since it tells **which one** and it describes a noun, it is an **adjective** phrase. It modifies the object of the preposition—*corner.* Diagram it like this:

Quick Tip

Remember the diagram position of the indirect object.

He gave Jake a gift.

The diagrams for indirect objects and prepositional phrases are very similar. Because the indirect object tells *to whom, for whom,* or *to what, for what* about the verb, this similarity is logical. *He gave the gift to Jake* is another way to say *He gave Jake a gift.* If the sentence actually contained the prepositional phrase *to Jake* instead of an indirect object, the diagram frame would look the same. The only difference would be the inclusion of the preposition on the diagonal line.

Indirect object   Prepositional phrase

PRACTICE SET 4–5

Directions: In the sentences below, place each prepositional phrase in parentheses and write it in the blank. Next, determine the word that each phrase modifies and the function of the phrase as an adjective or an adverb. Then, on a separate sheet of paper, diagram the sentence.

Example: The capital (of Idaho) is Boise.

Prepositional phrase: _____ of Idaho _____

Word it modifies: _____ capital _____

Prepositional phrase functions as: _____ adjective _____

```
capital  |  is  \  Boise
 \  \              
 The \ of
       Idaho
```

1. On Tuesday, I have three classes.

   Prepositional phrase: _____

   Word it modifies: _____

   Prepositional phrase functions as: _____

2. They discontinued the search for the missing pilot after ten days.

   Prepositional phrase: _____

   Word it modifies: _____

   Prepositional phrase functions as: _____

   Prepositional phrase: _____

   Word it modifies: _____

   Prepositional phrase functions as: _____

3. My best friend from camp arrived by train.

   Prepositional phrase: _____

   Word it modifies: _____

   Prepositional phrase functions as: _____

Prepositional phrase: _____

Word it modifies: _____

Prepositional phrase functions as: _____

4. The Devil Rays played a double-header at Tropicana Field on Sunday afternoon.

Prepositional phrase: _____

Word it modifies: _____

Prepositional phrase functions as: _____

Prepositional phrase: _____

Word it modifies: _____

Prepositional phrase functions as: _____

5. The hamster slept soundly on a towel in the closet.

Prepositional phrase: _____

Word it modifies: _____

Prepositional phrase functions as: _____

Prepositional phrase: _____

Word it modifies: _____

Prepositional phrase functions as: _____

Optional Practice

PRACTICE SET 4–6

Directions: On a separate sheet of paper, diagram the following sentences.

Example: The little girl from Kansas arrived in Oz.

1. The telephone on the desk rang loudly.

2. I broke my leg on Wednesday.

3. The movie about the Alamo stars two actors from Texas.

4. I cut the hedges with a sharp hedge trimmer.

5. The theater at Westshore Mall opened today.

6. The pigeon under the park bench looks sick.

7. The photographer for the *New York Times* hid behind a tree.

8. The fire spread from the top floor of the building.

9. People like him never understand people like us.

10. The president of the company read the poem at the bottom of the page.

Verb Phrases

So far, verbs have been single words, but they can also be phrases. A **verb phrase** consists of a main verb and its auxiliary (helping) verbs:

Forms of *to be:*	am, is, are, was, were, be, being, been
Forms of *to have:*	has, have, had
Forms of *to do:*	do, does, did
Modals:	may, might, can, could, shall, should, will, would, must

Quick Tip

The auxiliary verbs that show necessity (*must*), ability (*can, could*), permission or possibility (*may, might*), promise, determination, or intention (*shall, should, will, would*) are called **modals.** Modals are verbs that do not have infinitive or participial forms, but they are always part of a verb phrase.

A verb phrase may include one auxiliary verb plus a main verb:

AV MV

He *is singing* a song.

It can also include several auxiliary verbs.

AV   AV   AV   MV

She *should have been exercising* daily.

PRACTICE SET 4–7

Directions: Double-underline the verb phrases in the following sentences.

Example: Margarite <u>should have arrived</u> by now.

1. Mr. Herriot will file those papers immediately.

2. You should practice before your lesson.

3. They are committing a crime.

4. I have asked him a personal question.

5. Larry would have been thirty-five today.

6. He might do me a favor.

7. Marcos could have been playing quarterback this year.

8. Ariana can help you with the party.

9. I am offering you a tremendous discount.

10. She has had a string of unfortunate accidents.

Quick Tip

Frequently, adverbs appear within the verb phrase. Do not identify them as part of the verb phrase. Consider this sentence:

He *is* always *telling* stupid jokes.

Is telling is the verb phrase, and *always* is an adverb describing when he is telling the jokes. Be particularly careful about the word *not*.

He *has* not *been doing* his homework.

The verb phrase is *has been doing*. *Not* tells how he has been doing. Thus, it is an adverb, not part of the verb. Don't forget that *n't* is the contraction for *not* and is not part of the verb phrase.

He *wasn't telling* the truth.

The verb phrase is simply *was telling*.

PRACTICE SET 4–8

Directions: Double-underline the verb phrases in the following sentences.

Example: Harvey <u>should</u> not <u>have answered</u> so quickly.

1. Jessica would never break her promise to you.

2. I have not told anyone your secret.

3. I have just sold my first painting.

4. He wouldn't have given you the money.

5. They should never have been swimming in that dangerous area.

6. Everett is still waiting for his refund check.

7. This spy story can't possibly be true.

8. The twins have never had the chance to know their father.

9. The child shouldn't be sitting on the wet grass.

10. Allison is always bragging about her children.

Quick Tip

In Chapter 2, you learned to distinguish between adjectives that follow linking verbs (*The magician is **amazing***) and verb phrases (*The magician **is amazing** the audience*). To determine whether the word following a form of the verb *to be* is part of the verb phrase or is a subject complement, remember to ask yourself whether it shows action or describes the subject.

> Joseph Dover was married.

Married describes Joseph Dover; thus the verb is *was*, and *married* is a subject complement.

> Joseph Dover married Janice Fox.

Married shows action, so it is a verb. *Janice Fox* is the direct object.

PRACTICE SET 4–9

Directions: Indicate whether the word in boldface is a subject complement because it describes the subject or is part of the verb because it shows action.

Examples:

My new pen is **missing.**   *Describes—subject complement*

She is really **missing** her mother.   *Shows action—verb*

1. The doctor **worried** about his patient's recovery. _____

2. My mother was **worried** about my car accident. _____

3. They have **gone** to the mountains to ski. _____

4. Elvis is **gone** but not forgotten.   _____

5. The mystery play is **surprising** the audience.   _____

6. Your offer is really **surprising.**   _____

7. I knew at once that the game was **lost.**   _____

8. She **lost** her sweater at the movies.   _____

9. We have **exhausted** our water supply.   _____

10. The runners are really **exhausted.**   _____

Diagramming Verb Phrases

The entire verb phrase is placed in the verb position on the diagram frame. Examine this sentence:

> He is doing his homework.

In this sentence, the complete verb is the verb phrase *is doing*. To diagram this sentence, you must put the entire verb phrase in the verb position of the diagram frame.

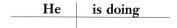

He is doing what? He is doing his homework, so *homework* is the direct object. *His* is an adjective modifying *homework*. The completed diagram looks like this:

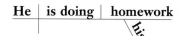

Here is another sentence:

> He may have been wrong.

To diagram this sentence, put the entire verb phrase in the verb position of the diagram frame. Since *may have been* is a form of the verb *to be*, it is a linking verb; therefore, *wrong* appears in the subject complement position.

He | may have been \ wrong

PRACTICE SET 4–10

Directions: Double-underline all verb phrases in the following sentences. Then diagram the sentences. Remember not to include as part of the verb modifiers found within verb phrases.

Example: Martin is not running the business successfully.

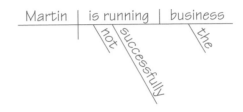

1. William is always giving me an excuse.

2. Beverly was being unusually quiet today.

3. Richard's speech has not been very interesting.

4. They are certainly succeeding in their efforts.

5. Micki had never fallen before.

6. The dance troupe is appearing at the theater over the weekend.

7. Robin might have been the winner.

8. Sigfried is seeing his stockbroker today.

9. Mr. Burke has been divorced for two years.

10. Julie has never hired a babysitter for her daughter.

Appositive Phrases

An **appositive** renames a noun or a pronoun. It usually follows the noun and identifies, explains, or supplements the meaning of the noun. An **appositive phrase** consists of the appositive and its modifiers.

noun   modifier modifier appositive
Stephanie, my   oldest daughter, left for college today.

noun   appositive
Ernest Hemingway wrote the novel *For Whom the Bell Tolls.*

(The entire title acts as the appositive.)

To diagram an appositive phrase, place the appositive in parentheses in the same position as the noun it renames, its modifiers beneath it.

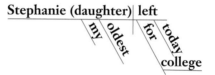

An appositive or an appositive phrase can appear next to a noun in any position in the sentence.

Appositive with subject: Dr. Rockwell, my dentist, has office hours on weekends.

Appositive with object of the preposition:

I left the package with   Mr. Foxworth,   the doorman.

Appositive with direct object: I was playing Hearts, a card game.

Appositive with indirect object: I gave Shelly, my girlfriend, a single rose.

Appositive with subject complement: He is our leader, the man in charge.

Appositive with object complement: We called her Sammy, a family nickname.

PRACTICE SET 4–11

Directions: Circle the appositive phrases in the sentences below. Then diagram the sentences.

Example: I offered Mrs. Gale, (the secretary,) an apology.

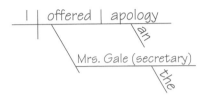

1. Mrs. Dumeyer, my drama coach, is starring in a new play.

2. The award goes to Valerie Muñoz, our most valuable player.

3. The character Hagrid appears in *Harry Potter and the Sorcerer's Stone.*

4. Kwanzaa, an African-American cultural festival, is celebrated in December.

5. She is the winner, the fastest runner in the school.

6. I invited Michael, my best friend, to the party.

7. The movie tells the story of the *Titanic,* the doomed ship.

8. The judge gave Ted, my supervisor, a suspended sentence.

9. Judy Garland starred in the movie *The Wizard of Oz.*

10. Max's is my favorite restaurant, the best steak place in town.

TEST YOURSELF

Directions: In each blank at the right, indicate whether the underlined phrase is a prepositional phrase, a verb phrase, or an appositive phrase.

Example: I <u>have been thinking</u> about summer vacation.   *verb phrase*

1. Many electrical cords are needed <u>for a new computer hook-up.</u>   _____

2. Monet, <u>an impressionist painter</u>, experimented with reflected light.   _____

3. After my doctor's appointment <u>on Wednesday</u>, I will go back to work.   _____

4. When we heard the siren, we knew the time <u>of real danger</u> was over.   _____

5. Smitty <u>has never seen</u> a live manatee.   _____

6. Mother <u>has been donating</u> most of her spare time to charity.   _____

7. The movie <u>*Prince of Egypt*</u> is based on a story in the Hebrew Bible.   _____

8. <u>During the frog dissection demonstration</u>, Sylvia had to leave the room.   _____

9. Chalkboards <u>have been replaced</u> by whiteboards.   _____

10. <u>For the last ten years</u>, he hid his money under his mattress.   _____

COMPOSITION WARM-UP

Directions: Add phrases to the sentences below.

Add appositives:

1. Cousin Wilbur, _____, will not be coming to the reunion this year.

2. A careless shopper backed into my new car, _____.

3. Lourdes Montego, _____, gave an exciting speech about her wilderness vacation.

4. Istanbul, _____, has the largest open-air market in the world.

5. I forwarded the memo to Sophie Moss, _____.

Add verb phrases:

6. The Help the Children Campaign _____ $25,000 by the end of the month.

7. Ellie _____ on the phone for two hours.

Add prepositional phrases:

8. _____, I prefer to eat a hearty breakfast of whole grains, fruit, and yogurt.

9. _____, my boyfriend gave me a box _____.

10. Sean found a diamond bracelet _____.

COMPOSITION PRACTICE

Directions: Write five sentences about a favorite movie or television show. Include an appositive, a verb phrase, or a prepositional phrase in each sentence.

WORD WATCHERS

Some words sound alike but have very different meanings. Be sure to use the words that you mean.

fewer/less	If you count them, use *fewer*; if you weigh or measure them, use *less:* There are fewer roses on the bush this year because I used less fertilizer.
lead/led	*Lead,* rhyming with *bead,* means *to go in front:* Martin wants to lead the parade.
	Its past tense is *led:* Yesterday, Martin led the parade.
	Lead, rhyming with *head,* is a metal: The fisherman used a lead sinker on his line.

(continued)

WORD WATCHERS
(cont.)

loose/lose *Loose* means *not tight*. It rhymes with *goose*. When you *lose* something, you can't find it: If my bracelet is too loose, it may fall off, and I will lose it.

number/amount If you count it, use *number*; if you weigh or measure it, use *amount*. This is the same rule as *fewer/less:* A small number of students used a large amount of paint.

passed/past *Passed* is the past tense of the verb *pass:* I passed my test with flying colors.

Past can be a noun referring to an earlier time: In the past, women wore corsets and hoop skirts.

Past can be an adjective describing something or someone from an earlier time: Our past president is resigning from the club.

Past can be an adverb: We drove past.

Past can be a preposition: They walked past the house.

WORD WATCHERS PRACTICE SET

Directions: Choose the correct word in the parentheses.

1. Try not to (loose/lose) all of your money when you go to Las Vegas.

2. Marguerite (lead/led) the class in the Pledge of Allegiance.

3. The (number/amount) of oranges on my tree has doubled since the weather turned warm.

4. On my way to work this morning, I (passed/past) the house where I used to live.

5. You can check out in the express lane if you have ten items or (fewer/less).

6. I lost my earring because the back was (loose/lose).

7. There are (fewer/less) typos in this paragraph than in your previous one.

8. Superman cannot see through anything made of (lead/led).

9. Emma was afraid to marry him because of his troubled (passed/past).

10. I will follow wherever you (lead/led).

Chapter 5

Verbals and Verbal Phrases

Verbals are words that are formed from verbs but that do not function as verbs. Because verbals come from verbs, they look like verbs, but a word cannot be a verb and a verbal at the same time.

There are three types of verbals: participles, gerunds, and infinitives.

Participles

Participles function as adjectives. Present participles end in *-ing* (*singing*); past participles usually end in *-ed* (*excited*), *-t* (*built*), *-k* (*drunk*), or *-n* (*eaten*). Because participles function as adjectives, they usually appear next to the noun or pronoun they modify.

> The *singing* waiter entertained my mother.

> The *excited* child opened his presents.

Sometimes it is difficult to differentiate a participle from the main verb of the sentence. *Singing* sounds like a verb. However, if you carefully examine the phrase *the singing waiter*, you notice that *waiter* is a noun and *singing* is an adjective that tells **what kind** of waiter. Thus, it is a **verbal,** not a verb. The verb in the sentence is *entertained*.

A **participial phrase** is a phrase that contains a participle and the words that go with it.

> The player *wearing the red shirt* was obviously the fastest.

The phrase *wearing the red shirt* tells **which one** about *the player*.

> *Arriving late,* the bride slipped past the guests in the lobby.

This one is trickier, for it might be hard to see that *arriving late* is an adjective, just like *wearing the red shirt*. **What kind** of bride? An *arriving late* bride.

PRACTICE SET 5–1

Directions: In the sentences below, circle the nouns or pronouns modified by the participles and participial phrases in boldface.

Example: We saw a frustrated (mother) **running after her child.**

1. The attorney based his case on **proven** information.

2. The museum **showing the new Dalí exhibit** stayed open until midnight.

3. **Walking too quickly into the cage,** the zookeeper startled the lioness.

4. Lazy campers leave **littered** sites.

5. **Knowing his travel schedule,** we planned a welcome-home party.

PRACTICE SET 5–2

Directions: Underline all of the participles or participial phrases in the sentences below. Then circle the nouns or pronouns they modify. A sentence may have more than one participle or participial phrase.

Example: The fallen (soldier) lay motionless on the battlefield.

1. Following my instructions, someone left the package on the doorstep.

2. I saw the half-eaten sandwich next to the television.

3. The photograph bearing his signature is worth a lot of money.

4. During the raging storm, he comforted the frightened child.

5. He called to the police officer standing by the cruiser.

6. Built in 1911, this building has been condemned.

7. Lisa stopped to talk to the frustrated man selling his paintings at the art fair.

8. Worried about his grade, he made an appointment with his professor.

9. The short story written by Alice Walker won the coveted award.

10. The smiling project manager showed the boss her finished product.

Gerunds

Gerunds always end in -*ing*, but unlike participles, they function as nouns.

Studying is important.

The gerund *studying* is the subject of the sentence. **Gerund phrases** consist of the gerund and the words that go with it.

Studying the lesson is important.

To decide whether an -*ing* word is a gerund or a participle, try to identify its function in the sentence.

Gerunds act as nouns, so think about where you would find a noun in a sentence. Nouns can be **subjects, direct objects, indirect objects, subject complements,** or **objects of a preposition.** These basic sentence parts usually cannot be taken out of the sentence. Likewise, because gerunds function as these basic sentence parts, the gerund phrase usually cannot be taken out of the sentence.

Participles act as adjectives. They tell **which one, what kind,** or **how many** about a noun or pronoun. Because adjectives are simply modifiers, participles can always be left out of the sentence.

Try the "leave-out" test with these two sentences.

Driving in the rain can be dangerous.

Driving in the rain, she became nervous.

In the first sentence, the -*ing* phrase is a gerund functioning as the subject. If you leave it out, the sentence is incomplete. In the second sentence, the -*ing* phrase is a participle modifying the subject *she*. If you leave it out, the sentence, although not as detailed, is still complete.

Once you have decided that an -*ing* phrase is a gerund, look at it in relation to the main verb of the sentence. Then consider the sentence patterns (see Chapter 2) and determine where the gerund fits in.

Subject:	*Writing an essay* requires concentration.
Direct object:	He enjoys *cooking gourmet meals for his family.*
Indirect object:	He gave *training for the marathon* his total effort.
Subject complement:	His lifelong dream is *traveling around the world.*
Object of the preposition:	Before *setting the table,* you should wash your hands.

PRACTICE SET 5–3

Directions: In the following sentences, indicate the functions of the gerunds and gerund phrases in boldface. Indicate whether they are subjects, direct objects, indirect objects, subject complements, or objects of prepositions.

Example: **Soaking in a hot tub** is relaxing
after a long day at work.   *subject*

1. **Selling Cuban cigars** is illegal.   _____

2. He enjoys **singing in the shower.**   _____

3. After **receiving a gift,** you should send
   a thank-you note.   _____

4. He got a blister from **walking so far.**   _____

5. A noble pursuit is **seeking the truth.**   _____

6. I really love **wrapping Christmas presents.**   _____

7. Her main objective was **getting good grades
   in English.**   _____

8. I don't like **answering the telephone.**   _____

9. **Keeping alert during class** is sometimes difficult.   _____

10. Mr. Smithers gave **planting his garden** all of
    his free time.   _____

PRACTICE SET 5–4

Directions: Identify the phrases in boldface as gerunds or participles. If the phrase in boldface is a gerund, indicate its use as subject, direct object, indirect object, subject complement, or object of a preposition. If the phrase in boldface is a participial phrase, identify the noun it modifies.

Examples:

Watching the bug, the kitten began
to purr.   *participle—modifies kitten*

Ironing the shirt took a long time.   *gerund—subject*

1. **Bowing gracefully,** the handsome
   dancer enjoyed the applause.   _____

2. This unusual vase, **crafted by hand,**
   is very expensive.   _____

3. **Selling everything cheaply** was
   important to him.   _____

4. Elena does not mind **lending the money.**   _____

5. The two spaniels **sleeping peacefully by the fire** did not bother the burglar.   _____

6. You can make a lot of money through **investing carefully.**   _____

7. **Developed by a team of surgeons,** the new procedure saved Evan's life.   _____

8. **Losing ten pounds** is my goal for this month.   _____

9. I found my missing jacket by **cleaning my closet.**   _____

10. **Sentenced to ten years in prison,** Arnie showed no signs of remorse.   _____

Infinitives

Infinitives begin with *to*, followed by the base form of the verb. **Infinitive phrases** include the infinitive and the words that go with it. Infinitives and infinitive phrases function as nouns, adjectives, or adverbs.

Infinitives as Nouns

When infinitives are used as nouns, they act as either subjects, direct objects, subject complements, or objects of prepositions.

Infinitive phrase as subject: *To answer my question* took an hour.

Infinitive phrase as direct object: I like *to read in bed.*

Infinitive phrase as subject complement: My goal is *to make money.*

Infinitive phrase as object of a preposition: Except *to visit the doctor,* the old woman rarely left home.

Infinitives as Adjectives

When infinitives are used as adjectives, they modify nouns or pronouns and tell **which one, what kind,** or **how many.**

Infinitive phrase modifying a noun: The rent *to be paid in April* was late.

Infinitive phrase modifying a pronoun: He was always looking for someone *to blame.*

Infinitives as Adverbs

When infinitives are used as adverbs, they modify verbs, adjectives, or other adverbs, and they tell **where, when, why, how,** or **to what extent.**

Infinitive phrase modifying a verb:	*To catch a butterfly,* use a net.
Infinitive phrase modifying an adjective:	You are right *to complain.*
Infinitive phrase modifying an adverb:	He ran too slowly *to win the race.*

Is it a prepositional phrase or an infinitive?

to plus a **noun** = prepositional phrase: I went *to* **school.**
to plus a **verb** = infinitive: I like *to* **sing.**

PRACTICE SET 5–5

Directions: Indicate whether the infinitive phrases in boldface act as nouns, adjectives, or adverbs. If they are nouns, indicate their function in the sentence.

Examples:

To check your work, add each
column separately.   *adverb*

She seems **to like her job.**   *noun—subject complement*

1. I need **to buy a new coat.**   _____

2. **To understand people,** you should put
   yourself in their shoes.   _____

3. **To be loved** is the most important
   quality of all.   _____

4. My quest is **to dream the impossible
   dream.**   _____

5. I want **to have a good time.**   _____

6. The movie **to see tonight** is *Gone with
   the Wind.*   _____

7. **To receive your refund quickly,** you
   must submit a receipt.   _____

8. **To win the game** is not always possible. _____

9. Our plan is **to surprise her.**   _____

10. The dress **to be cleaned** is hanging on the rack.   _____

PRACTICE SET 5–6

Directions: Identify the words in boldface as verbs or verbals. If they are verbals, indicate whether they are participles, gerunds, or infinitives.

Examples:

The **laughing** toddler made everyone smile.   *verbal—participle*

The toddler was **laughing.**   *verb*

1. The old man had such **wrinkled** skin.   _____

2. I **wrinkled** the paper and threw it in the trash.   _____

3. Horseback **riding** is a lot of fun.   _____

4. The jockey was **riding** a sure winner.   _____

5. This campsite has **running** water.   _____

6. He is **running** a great campaign.   _____

7. I love **to run** in cold weather.   _____

8. **Running** in place, Jan sprained her ankle.   _____

9. **To record** a message, please wait for the tone.   _____

10. Before **recording** a message, wait for the tone.   _____

11. A **recorded** message is sometimes hard to understand.   _____

12. He **recorded** the message carefully.   _____

13. The **recording** artist won a Grammy.   _____

14. **Recording** a message, Mike left the information and hung up. _____

15. I am **recording** my message for you. _____

COMPOSITION WARM-UP

Directions: Underline all verbals and verbal phrases in the following paragraphs, and label them as participles, gerunds, or infinitives.

Arturo Sandoval, one of the most celebrated jazz musicians of our time, was born near Havana, Cuba, in 1949. His early training was as a classical musician, but at age twelve, upon hearing his first jazz recordings, he knew that he wanted to be a jazz trumpeter. A founding member of Irakere, a band blending traditional Latin sounds with jazz, rock, and classical music, Sandoval tried to explore new musical territory but was frequently censored by the Castro regime. Aided by jazz great Dizzy Gillespie, Sandoval defected to the United States in 1990. His wife and son joined him later.

Nominated twelve times for Grammies and awarded three, Sandoval continues to excite music lovers throughout the world. Cuban-born actor Andy Garcia, fascinated by his countryman's amazing life, wanted to tell Sandoval's story to the world. He was able to do so in November 2000, when he starred in an HBO television movie entitled *For Love or Country: The Arturo Sandoval Story.*

TEST YOURSELF

Directions: Underline all the verbals and verbal phrases in the following sentences. Label each one as *P* for participle, *G* for gerund, or *I* for infinitive.

                    G   *P*

Example: <u>Knitting a sweater</u> is a <u>forgotten</u> art.

1. Anticipating an accident, he swerved away from the approaching car.

2. My pressing dilemma is whether to sign the contract now or to wait until next year.

3. The swollen river rose two feet a day, overflowing its banks.

4. Exhausted from the drive, the college student decided to stop at a motel.

5. Mastering the game of chess takes hours of concentrated effort.

6. Her accumulated wealth increased her ability to help needy children.

7. Singing arias gave the trained tenor the practice that he needed.

8. Eating healthy foods can lead to a prolonged life.

9. Avoiding tobacco and alcohol improved his condition.

10. Avoiding tobacco and alcohol, he was able to improve his condition.

COMPOSITION PRACTICE

Directions: Write five sentences on *one* of the following topics:

a. annoying things that drivers do

b. ways to stay on a diet

c. things I would change about my job

Use either a participle, a gerund, or an infinitive in each sentence. These verbals may occur alone or in phrases. Underline each verbal or verbal phrase.

WORD WATCHERS

Some words sound alike but have very different meanings. Be sure to use the words that you mean.

principal/principle   *Principal* has three meanings. It refers to the leader of the school: Mrs. Cunningham is the principal of Ballast Point Elementary School.

(continued)

WORD WATCHERS
(*cont.*)

It means the chief or main anything: My principal reason for leaving is clear.

It refers to the money that generates interest: He spends only the interest, never the principal.

Principle has two meanings. It means a fundamental truth or law: The principles of gravity never change.

It also means morals or standards for living: He is a man of high principles.

stationery/stationary   *Stationery* is writing paper: I wrote him a letter on my best stationery.

Stationary means *motionless:*   The hunter remained stationary as the tiger approached.

then/than   *Then* is an adverb telling when: I drank my coffee, and then I paid the bill.

Than is a subordinating conjunction that introduces a comparison: Millie is smarter than Paco.

to/too/two   *To* has two functions. *To* is a preposition: I followed him to the cafeteria.

To is also part of an infinitive: I don't want to insult you.

Too is an adverb meaning *also:*   Ellie has a brother too.

Too also adds intensity to adjectives: This sauce is too hot to eat.

Two is a number: Owen has two teeth missing.

whether/weather   *Whether* is a subordinating conjunction that suggests a choice: We will hold the race whether it rains or not.

Weather is a noun referring to atmospheric conditions: We held the race despite the bad weather.

WORD WATCHERS PRACTICE SET

Directions: Choose the correct word in the parentheses.

1. The mourners remained (stationery/stationary) while the funeral procession passed.

2. It is (to/too) cold outside to wear short sleeves.

3. A new Lexus usually costs more (then/than) a new Chevy.

(*continued*)

WORD WATCHERS
(cont.)

4. My (principal/principle) responsibility on this job is to assure product safety.

5. I have not yet told you (whether/weather) I intend to vote for you.

6. The rules for baseball and softball are different, but the (principals/principles) are the same.

7. The Chief Justice of the Supreme Court offered an opinion (to/too).

8. When you pay down your mortgage, the interest is deducted before the (principal/principle).

9. After she moved, I gave her a box of (stationary/stationery) with her new address printed on it.

10. We should always live according to our (principals/principles).

Chapter 6

Word Order Variations

In the usual order of words in a sentence, the subject comes first, followed by the verb and then any complements. However, this word order has some important exceptions, which will be explained in this chapter.

Questions

Questions may invert the subject/verb order or place the subject between two parts of the verb. Note what happens to the subject when the following statement changes to a question:

> John is singing a solo in the senior recital.

> Is John singing a solo in the senior recital?

The first sentence follows a common Subject/Verb/Direct Object sentence pattern, but the second sentence, now a question, places the subject *John* between the two parts of the verb *is singing*. The subject and verb have not changed—only their positions have.

The best way to identify the sentence parts of a question is to turn the question into a statement.

> *Do* we *have* something to contribute?

> We *do have* something to contribute.

> *Will* you *paint* the kitchen?

> You *will paint* the kitchen.

PRACTICE SET 6–1

Directions: Change the following questions into statements and underline the verbs twice and the subjects once.

Example: Do you remember my name? You do remember my name.

1. Have we discovered a new technique?

2. Did the police officer issue him a ticket?

3. May I offer you a lift?

4. Has the mail arrived?

5. Should we practice before our performance?

There is/are and *There was/were*

The word *there* frequently introduces a sentence, functioning simply as an adverb or an introductory word—not the subject. In fact, the word *there* often causes the subject to follow the verb.

Always look beyond the *there* to find the subject because the word *there* is never the subject.

        V   S
There *are* three banana *muffins* in the refrigerator.

        V   S
There *was someone* in the car with her.

PRACTICE SET 6–2

Directions: In the following sentences, underline the verbs twice and the subjects once.

Example: There on the couch sat Henry.

1. There is no paper in the copier.

2. There were three officers on duty during the midnight shift.

3. There is that new girl from Nigeria.

4. There was an eerie silence after the crash.

5. There goes the last bus to the mall.

Whenever possible, avoid using *there is/there are* constructions. They usually add unnecessary words to the sentence.

Wordy: There was a bug in my bed.

Concise: A bug was in my bed.

Commands and Requests

Commands and requests generally don't include an obvious subject. In these types of sentences, the subject is often the implied word *you*.

Take out the garbage!

Please forgive me.

The actual subject in these sentences is *you*, but the subject *you* is understood, not written.

PRACTICE SET 6–3

Directions: Write the subjects and verbs of the following sentences in the appropriate blanks. Because the subject is understood, not stated, put it in parentheses.

Example: Please mail your payment on time.

Subject: (you)   Verb: mail

1. Never carry your wallet in your back pocket.

Subject: _____   Verb: _____

2. Always read the fine print before using a credit card.

Subject: _____   Verb: _____

3. Take your friend to the new theater in City Center.

Subject: _____   Verb: _____

4. After a workout, relax with a cool-down period.

Subject: _____   Verb: _____

5. Study the dates for the history test.

Subject: _____   Verb: _____

PRACTICE SET 6–4

Directions: Underline the verb twice and the subject once. If the sentence is a command, add the understood *you*.

Examples:

Will you attend the state fair?

(You) Sign your name on the dotted line.

1. There are no excuses for this lengthy delay.

2. Where does the Ganges River flow?

3. Buy the tickets for the play in advance.

4. There is a very good reason for his decision.

5. Always check the oil in your car before a trip.

6. Did Carmen raise her hand during class?

7. There is magic in the air.

8. Will the mercury rise above freezing tonight?

9. Send your mother flowers for Mother's Day.

10. Do not put your elbows on the table during dinner.

TEST YOURSELF

Directions: Underline the verb twice and the subject once. If the sentence is a command, add the understood *you*.

Examples: Do you want fries with your order?

(You) Give me a dollar to pay the tip.

1. Never leave the dryer running when you are not at home.

2. Will Karen find the message on her bulletin board?

3. Why did Josef cancel his flight?

4. There are no limes on the tree.

5. Offer your enemies your hand in friendship.

6. Please do not leave your station unattended.

7. There is only one reason for the delay.

8. How do these photographs compare with the ones from last week?

9. Should we taste the sauce before serving it?

10. Tell me the truth.

COMPOSITION WARM-UP

Directions: Rewrite the following sentences, avoiding the "there is/there are" construction.

1. There are many people who refuse to wait in line for anything.

2. I am unhappy when there are too many choices.

3. I can see that there is no alternative.

4. The instructor remains after class whenever there are questions.

5. Please let me know if there is too much salt in the stew.

6. There is a reason for his behavior.

7. Gavin will call me if there is a problem.

8. I noticed there were flaws in the plan.

9. Where there is smoke, there is fire.

10. I left early because there was a power outage.

COMPOSITION PRACTICE

Directions: Write five sentences describing your classroom. Do not use a "there is" or "there are" construction in any sentence.

WORD WATCHERS

Sometimes, instead of thinking hard to find the words that say what they mean, some writers carelessly include trite, overused words or phrases that may not make sense. Choose your words carefully.

and etc.	*Et cetera* is a Latin phrase meaning *and others*. If you say "And etc.," you are really saying, "And and others." Do not use the *and* with *et cetera*. Avoid using *etc.* in formal writing.
could care less	Saying that you *could* care less means that you do care—you aren't caring as little as you could because you could still care less. If you mean that you *don't* care, you should say, "I could **not** care less."
hopefully	*Hopefully* is an adverb that means "in a hopeful manner": He bought his lotto ticket hopefully. It should not be used in place of "I hope," as in "Hopefully, it will not rain today."
since the beginning of time	Unless you are a physicist who is truly referring to "the beginning of time" or making a biblical reference, this is a poor phrase to use to express how long something has been going on. Everyone—biblical scholars and scientists—seem to agree that there were no people in the beginning of time.
in today's society	There is no one society of "today." Use just *today* or specify the society that you mean: Today, viewers can choose from many television channels.
very unique	*Unique* means "one of a kind." Something cannot be "very" one of a kind. Use *unique* without the qualifier *very*.

WORD WATCHERS PRACTICE SET

Directions: Rewrite the following sentences, improving any carelessly written phrases.

1. They have been dating since the beginning of the universe.

2. She is a little bit pregnant.

(continued)

WORD WATCHERS
(*cont.*)

3. I'm dying to meet the drummer in that band.

4. Hopefully, the baby will go to sleep, and I will be able to watch the basketball game.

5. We packed just the important items: food, water, warm clothing, blankets, and etc.

6. He tried to interest her in the brushes he was selling, but she could have cared less.

7. In today's society, it is very important to keep abreast of world events.

8. Markie, who hadn't eaten since breakfast that morning, told his mother that he was absolutely starving.

9. This strange-looking bird is very unique.

10. She was very laid back in her attitude.

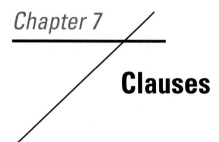

Chapter 7

Clauses

A **clause** is a group of related words containing a subject and a verb. In this chapter, you will learn about two basic kinds of clauses: independent and dependent clauses.

Independent Clauses

An **independent clause** is another name for a complete sentence.

The motorcycle skidded across the road.

The plant on the front porch died.

Dependent Clauses

A **dependent clause** cannot stand alone as a sentence. Even though it has a subject and a verb, it is not complete. It depends on the rest of the sentence to complete the thought. The following clauses have subjects and verbs, but they do not complete a thought.

When the motorcycle skidded across the road . . .

After the plant on the front porch died . . .

. . . that bother me.

Whoever wants to leave early . . .

If I do not come back by noon . . .

Dependent clauses never stand alone as a sentence. Notice how these clauses fit into complete sentences:

When the motorcycle skidded, the driver steered it safely.

After the plant on the front porch died, I replaced it with an artificial one.

There are two things *that bother me* about my girlfriend.

Whoever wants to leave early must fill out a form.

If I do not come back by noon, you may meet me at the mall.

> Never punctuate a dependent clause as if it were a complete sentence. Doing so creates a sentence fragment.
>
> dependent clause (fragment)
> Ricky did his laundry. *Because all of his socks were dirty.*
>
> Learn more about sentence fragments in Chapter 9.

Dependent clauses can function as adverbs, adjectives, or nouns.

Adverb Clauses

Dependent clauses that function as adverbs are usually easy to spot because they are introduced by special words called **subordinating conjunctions.** Listed below are some common subordinating conjunctions that introduce adverb clauses. For a complete list, see Chapter 16.

after	before	so that	when
although	if	than	whenever
as (as if, as though)	once	unless	wherever
because	since	until	while

Adverb clauses function like single-word adverbs. They usually modify verbs, but they can also modify adjectives and adverbs.

AC
Since the chairman was absent, I ran the meeting.

AC
Hungry *because we hadn't eaten since breakfast,* we stopped at the roadside diner.

AC
My brother works harder *than I do.*

Adverb clauses can appear at the beginning or end of a sentence, and they tell the following:

When: *While Lucy cleared the table,* Danny washed the dishes.

Where:	*Wherever you lead,* I will follow.
Why:	I stayed late *because he needed my help.*
How:	He cried *as though his heart would break.*
To what extent:	He ran *as far as he could.*

Adverb clauses exhibit two important characteristics:

- Adverb clauses always begin with a subordinating conjunction.

  SC
  Because I am tired, I cannot think clearly.

- Adverb clauses usually can change position in a sentence without changing the meaning.

  AC
  When I saw his face, I wept with joy.

  AC
  I wept with joy *when I saw his face.*

PRACTICE SET 7–1

Directions: In the sentences below, underline the adverb clauses.

Example: <u>If you follow the map,</u> you will find the buried treasure.

1. Crystal kept driving although the light had turned red.

2. Reuben runs faster than I do.

3. Because the fire continued to burn, the firefighters had to call for assistance.

4. He stared at me as if he knew me.

5. I will not answer him until he puts the question in writing.

6. Our sales are sure to decline because the interest rates have risen so quickly.

7. When the stock market crashed, many wealthy people experienced poverty for the first time.

8. Worried because I had not heard from him, I tried to reach him on my cell phone.

9. The Civil War began after the Confederates fired on Fort Sumter in 1861.

10. J. K. Rowling was on welfare before she published the first Harry Potter book.

 *Quick Tip*

A word can function as more than one part of speech. Many words can be both subordinating conjunctions and prepositions. A preposition is followed by its object—just a noun or pronoun and any modifiers. A subordinating conjunction is followed by a clause—a subject and a verb.

prepositional phrase
I studied   *until dawn.*

clause
I studied *until the sun rose.*

PRACTICE SET 7–2

Directions: Indicate whether the words in boldface are prepositional phrases or clauses.

Examples:

After the race, the runners needed water.   *prepositional phrase*

After Marnie left, we all voted on the issue.   *clause*

1. You must turn in your work **before you leave class.**   _____

2. You must turn in your work **before May.**   _____

3. She has been unemployed **since June.**   _____

4. She has been unemployed **since she lost her sales job.**   _____

5. **Until I got my test results,** I was worried about my health.   _____

6. **Until last week,** I was worried about my health.   _____

7. I will meet you **after the ceremony.**   _____

8. I will meet you **after the ceremony ends.**   _____

9. **Before the movie,** we went out to dinner.   _____

10. **Before we went to the movie,** we went out to dinner.   _____

Adjective Clauses

Like single-word adjectives, *adjective clauses* modify nouns and pronouns and tell the following:

Which one: The church *where we were married* has an enormous pipe organ.
(tells which church)

What kind: A cat *that scratches the furniture* should be kept outside.
(tells what kind of cat)

Listed below are some words that introduce adjective clauses.

who	whom	that	where
whose	which	when	why

She baked the cookies *that I liked*.

The town *where they live* has several colleges.

Unlike adverb clauses, adjective clauses cannot change position in the sentence. They directly follow the noun or pronoun that they modify, and moving them will change the meaning of the sentence or make it confusing.

Confusing: The runner showed his medal to the coach *who won the race*.

Clear: The runner who won the race showed his medal to the coach.

PRACTICE SET 7–3

Directions: In the sentences below, underline the adjective clauses. On the blank, write the word that the adjective clause modifies.

Example: The man who found my dog called me.   *man* _____

1. The violin that he plays is a real Stradivarius.   _____

2. Eunice searched for her glasses on the bench where she   _____
   had rested.

3. The reason that they left is obvious.   _____

4. The musician whom he had known became famous.   _____

5. This is a time when everyone must participate.   _____

6. Tonight's moon, which is really beautiful, is not full.   _____

7. Mrs. Roth, who turned ninety last week, still drives a car.   _____

8. Fortunately, the dog that bit Sammy did not have rabies.   _____

9. The place where we met was not very romantic.   _____

10. The artist whose work is displayed here died in 1950.   _____

Noun Clauses

Dependent clauses can function as nouns. They serve the same functions as single-word nouns or pronouns.

Subject: *How he could speak three languages fluently* really amazed me.

Direct object: Scott always says *whatever first comes into his mind.*

Indirect object: He offered *whoever washed his car* a ticket to the game.

Subject complement: The chairman will be *whomever the committee selects.*

Object of the preposition: This package is for *whoever wants it.*

Noun clauses exhibit several important characteristics:

- Noun clauses begin with one of the following words:

what	wherever	whoever	if
whatever	whether	whom	that
when	which	whomever	
whenever	whichever	why	
where	who	how	

- Because noun clauses serve as basic sentence parts, the sentences in which they appear are not complete without them. Examine the following sentence:

noun clause
Why he made that remark is unclear.

The noun clause *Why he made that remark* is the subject of the sentence. If you remove the clause, the sentence is incomplete.

Quick Tip

Since noun clauses function as main sentence parts, determining pronoun subjects can sometimes be confusing. Choose the pronoun according to its function in the clause, not according to the function of the clause in the sentence.

Whoever breaks the rules will be punished.

Whoever is the subject of the clause *whoever breaks the rules.* The clause *whoever breaks the rules* is the subject of the sentence.

I will give whoever fails the test a second chance.

Whoever is the subject of the clause *whoever fails the test.* The clause *whoever fails the test* is the indirect object of the sentence.

PRACTICE SET 7–4

Directions: In the following sentences, underline any noun clauses.

Example: I did not reveal <u>what you told me</u>.

1. I offered to trade my lunch for what she had brought.

2. Before President Roosevelt died, President Truman did not know that the United States was developing atomic weapons.

3. As the POWs sat in their makeshift cells, they didn't know if they could escape.

4. Where the *Titanic* rested remained a mystery for many decades.

5. We will promise whoever attends the gala a photo opportunity with the movie star.

6. We can understand why you chose to accept our offer.

7. The store gave refunds to whoever requested them.

8. The Red Cross promised the hurricane victims whatever they needed.

9. Whatever you wish is my command.

10. How she behaved was beyond belief.

PRACTICE SET 7–5

Directions: In the following sentences, indicate whether the dependent clauses in boldface are adjective, adverb, or noun clauses.

Example: Felix is the artist **who painted this picture.**   *adjective*

1. You should wash your hands **before you set the table.**   _____

2. I really appreciate a person **who is honest.**   _____

3. He is the man **whom I married.**   _____

4. My dog Flopsy, **who had puppies last month,** is a great mother.   _____

5. My father framed my award **because he was so proud of me.**   _____

6. You don't always tell me **what you need.**   _____

7. She cheered me up **when I was sad.**   _____

8. She mailed me the shirt **that I had left at her house.**   _____

9. **When the tornado struck,** we were in the basement.   _____

10. I knew **that he was truly sorry.**   _____

PRACTICE SET 7–6

Directions: Underline the dependent clauses in the sentences below.

Examples:

The story <u>that she read</u> was funny.

<u>Since I sold my car</u>, I have been riding the bus.

1. My computer, which has a virus, should be repaired.

2. Richard trimmed the tree that blocked my view.

3. She always gets whatever she wants.

4. What you do tonight will decide your fate.

5. The puppy tickled my toes while I was sleeping.

6. The house that they painted was really ugly.

7. Dante lost his keys when he was playing tennis.

8. The house where Mark Twain lived is now a museum.

9. If you forget the timer, you will burn the roast.

10. She bought the car that I wanted.

PRACTICE SET 7–7

Directions: In the paragraphs below, label the clauses in boldface as independent or dependent.

What happens to professional athletes **when their careers have ended? Once they leave the spotlight,** some find other rewarding careers. Others spend their lives playing imaginary games before adoring fans who exist only in memory. Alan Page is one athlete who knew from the start **that he did not want to sit on the sidelines of life.** An All-American defensive end for the Fighting Irish at Notre Dame in 1966, Page earned a degree in political science **before he became a**

first-round draft pick for the Minnesota Vikings in 1967. Page was the first defensive player ever to be named the NFL's Most Valuable Player, and **he was inducted into the Pro Football Hall of Fame on July 20, 1988.** These achievements, however, are the least important of Alan Page's remarkable life.

Page began planning for his life after football long **before the Vikings released him in 1978.** That same year, he graduated from the University of Minnesota Law School. After he served for six years as an assistant attorney general for the state of Minnesota, **Page was elected associate justice of the Minnesota Supreme Court in 1993. Although he was rarely "benched" as a football player,** Justice Page is happy to be on a different kind of bench today.

Justice Page speaks regularly to groups of minority students about the importance of education. He often addresses athletes who do not take advantage of the educational opportunities **that are available to them because of their athletic abilities.** He has said of such students: "We are doing no favors to the young men if we let them believe **that a game shall set them free."**

TEST YOURSELF

Directions: Underline the dependent clauses in the sentences below and indicate whether they are adjective, adverb, or noun clauses.

1. I don't understand what you are saying.

2. When Woodstock drew to a close, more than 450,000 people had gathered in the muddy pasture of Yasgur's farm.

3. Trees that shed their leaves before the cold or dry season are called deciduous trees.

4. Abraham Lincoln fired General McClellan because McClellan would not send the troops into battle.

5. The Bay of Pigs invasion of Cuba, which took place on April 17, 1961, was actually planned by President Eisenhower, but it became a political liability for President Kennedy.

6. The speaker gave whoever was making the racket a stern look.

7. She doesn't know where I am going.

8. Where you live dictates the type of clothing that you should purchase.

9. The corner where the accident occurred was closed to traffic for hours.

10. I will go wherever you go.

COMPOSITION WARM-UP

Directions: Fill in the blanks with the appropriate type of clause. Introductory words have been supplied for you.

1. *Adverb clause:* I left early **because** _____.

2. *Adverb clause:* **Although** _____, she found time to help me.

3. *Adverb clause:* They close the door **whenever** _____.

4. *Adjective clause:* The team **that** _____ will be eliminated in the next round.

5. *Adjective clause:* They tore down the movie theater **where** _____

   _____.

6. *Adjective clause:* The handyman **whom** _____ completed the job without charge.

7. *Adjective clause:* A dancer **whose** _____ must rest for at least one month.

8. *Noun clause:* Natalie didn't agree with **what** _____.

9. *Noun clause:* **Whoever** _____ will be responsible for turning out the lights.

10. *Noun clause:* I told her **that** _____.

COMPOSITION PRACTICE

Directions: Fill in the blanks with the appropriate type of clause. This time, you must supply the words that introduce the clauses. Remember that adverb clauses are introduced by subordinating conjunctions (*if, because, whenever, although, since, while*); adjective clauses are introduced by words like *who, whom, whose, which, that,*

why, where; noun clauses are introduced by words like *what, when, where, who, why, how, that.*

1. *Adverb clause:* _____, I try to remember to bring my umbrella.

2. *Adjective clause:* You should never try to keep animals _____ as pets.

3. *Noun clause:* I can't imagine _____.

4. *Noun clause:* She told him _____.

5. *Adjective clause:* The volunteer _____ raised $1,000 that evening.

6. *Adverb clause:* The general relieved the major from command _____

   _____.

7. *Adverb clause:* _____, I can lend you five dollars.

8. *Adjective clause:* Pookie hid in a place _____.

9. *Noun clause:* I gave the task to someone _____.

10. *Noun clause:* _____ is someone to wash the dishes.

WORD WATCHERS

Good writing is concise. Avoid using wordy expressions.

completely straight	By definition, something that is straight has no crooked parts. It is unnecessary to qualify *straight* with *completely.*
but yet	*But* and *yet* are coordinating conjunctions with the same meaning. Never use them together. Choose one or the other.
disappear from view	Something that disappears can no longer be seen. Adding *from view* is redundant.
self-inflicted suicide	*Suicide* is the act of taking one's own life. It must be self-inflicted, so adding the qualifier is unnecessary.
at this point in time	This is a wordy expression for *now.*

(continued)

WORD WATCHERS
(cont.)

refer back to

When you *refer*, you are already going back. Adding *back* is redundant.

WORD WATCHERS PRACTICE SET

Directions: Shorten the following phrases, eliminating wordiness.

1. green in color _____

2. made a motion _____

3. held a meeting _____

4. linked together _____

5. if it is at all possible _____

6. general consensus of opinion _____

7. made an announcement _____

8. arrived at the conclusion _____

9. at all times _____

10. came to a complete and total stop _____

Chapter 8

Types of Sentences

Classifying Sentences According to Purpose

There are several ways to classify sentences. One way is according to how the sentence expresses an idea.

A **declarative sentence** makes a statement:

My dog has fleas.

An **imperative sentence** commands or requests:

Exit the building quickly and quietly.

An **interrogative sentence** asks a question:

Have you met my mother?

An **exclamatory sentence** expresses emotion or strong feeling:

I simply cannot believe what I see!

Classifying Sentences According to Structure

Another important way to classify sentences is by the number of independent and dependent clauses they contain. In Chapter 7, you learned that an independent (or main) clause contains a subject and a verb and can stand alone as a sentence. A dependent (or subordinate) clause also contains a subject and a verb, but it cannot stand alone as a sentence.

Sentences may be classified as simple, compound, complex, and compound-complex.

Simple Sentences

The term *simple sentence* does not mean that a sentence is short or uncomplicated. A **simple sentence** contains only one clause, an independent clause. It may contain several modifying phrases. It may be short or long, easy or complicated, but it is still a simple sentence. Compare these two simple sentences:

S V
The dog barks.

S   V
The shaggy brown *dog* with the pretty pink ribbon around its neck *barks* noisily at the pesky squirrel climbing up the old oak tree in the park near the elementary school on Elm Street.

The second sentence has many modifying words and phrases, but because it contains only one independent clause and no dependent clauses, it is still a simple sentence.

PRACTICE SET 8–1

Directions: In the following simple sentences, underline the verb twice and the subject once.

Example: Jimmy Carter, the governor of Georgia, served as U.S. president from 1977 to 1981.

1. Andrew Jackson, the seventh president of the United States, once killed a man in a duel.

2. John Adams and Thomas Jefferson died on the same day, July 4, 1826.

3. James Buchanan was President James Polk's secretary of state and President Franklin Pierce's minister to Great Britain.

4. Dwight Eisenhower served as president of Columbia University following World War II.

5. Calvin Coolidge's father, a notary public, administered the oath of office to his son in 1923.

Compound Sentences

A **compound sentence** contains more than one independent clause and no dependent clauses. The independent clauses are joined by coordinating conjunctions or semicolons.

IC   CC   IC
Coordinating conjunction: I tried to fix my computer, but I was not successful.

IC   IC
Semicolon: Spring is my favorite season; the weather is always so beautiful.

Parts of Speech

Coordinating Conjunctions

Coordinating conjunctions connect sentence parts that are grammatically the same, such as two words, two phrases, or two clauses. There are seven coordinating conjunctions. Some people memorize them as a list: *and, but, or, for, nor, so, yet*. Others like to use a mnemonic (a memory aid), such as FANBOYS:

For
And
Nor
But
Or
Yet
So

Compound Subjects and Verbs

Certain types of sentences may appear to be compound when they really are not, so you must examine the structure carefully. Is this sentence a compound sentence?

$$\text{S} \qquad\qquad \text{S} \quad \text{V}$$
My algebra *teacher* and *Uncle Jack* are friends.

In this sentence, the coordinating conjunction *and* does not connect two independent clauses. It connects the two subjects of the sentence, *teacher* and *Uncle Jack*. This sentence contains a **compound subject.** It is a simple sentence, not a compound sentence. Now consider this sentence:

Milton *stood* in line and *paid* for the popcorn.

In this sentence, the coordinating conjunction *and* does not connect two independent clauses. It connects the two verbs, *stood* and *paid*. This sentence contains a **compound verb.** It is a simple sentence, not a compound sentence.

PRACTICE SET 8–2

Directions: In the following sentences, underline the verb twice and the simple subject once. Then indicate whether the sentences are simple or compound.

Examples: Keith circled the building and stopped at the front door.   *simple*

He withdrew $50 from his account, but he was still   *compound*
$10 short.

1. The sun, the nine planets and their moons, asteroids, comets, and meteors constitute our solar system. _____

2. Florida is the Sunshine State, but Georgia is the Peach State. _____

3. Making money in the stock market requires much research and a lot of luck. _____

4. Jenny Lind, the "Swedish Nightingale," toured the United States in 1850. _____

5. The copier and the fax machine are both out of order. _____

6. The poet Dante was really named Durante Alighieri; however, everyone remembers him simply as Dante. _____

7. Manny and I were both going to the same place, so I offered him a ride. _____

8. The clothes left on the ironing board and the jackets on the living room chair should be hung in the closet. _____

9. Neither the letter that I mailed on Tuesday nor the package that you sent on Wednesday has arrived yet. _____

10. Gelsey Kirkland attended the American School of Ballet, for she wanted to become a prima ballerina. _____

Complex Sentences

The term *complex sentence* has nothing to do with how complicated a sentence may appear. **Complex sentence** simply means that the sentence has only one independent clause and at least one dependent clause.

> DC
> *Because I could not stop in time*, I hit the garage door.

> DC
> Students *who like to read* usually do well in school.

> DC　　　IC
> *What you said* is not true.

Quick Tip Noun clauses may be difficult to spot because they are main parts of the independent clauses. Don't overlook them.

> noun clause as subject
> *When we meet* does not matter.

> noun clause as subject complement
> The miracle was *that he survived.*

PRACTICE SET 8–3

Directions: In the sentences below, underline all dependent clauses.

Example: You should always wear protective pads <u>when you rollerblade</u>.

1. Marie Curie, who worked with her husband, Pierre, won the Nobel Prize in physics for her work on radioactivity.

2. While he was working to improve the telegraph and telephone, Thomas Edison invented the phonograph in 1877.

3. I cannot believe how you managed to fool everyone.

4. Unhappy because she had ridiculed him, Walter sadly put the engagement ring back in its box.

5. Rooms that are cluttered with large furniture and knickknacks look small.

6. Where the plane crashed remains a mystery to the investigators.

7. The singer could not understand why everyone was leaving the room.

8. Hybrid cars, which combine power from gasoline and batteries, can cut fuel costs enormously.

9. Before you announce the results, be sure to check your facts.

10. The researchers made a discovery that changed the world forever.

PRACTICE SET 8–4

Directions: Identify the following sentences as simple, compound, or complex.

Examples:

The smog in the air is thick.	*simple*
She wants to travel, but she is afraid to fly.	*compound*
If you speak, I will listen.	*complex*

1. Randy fixed my computer, so now I can download music. _____

2. When you are finished, you may leave. _____

3. His jacket, which was wet, was hanging on the door. _____

4. Duchess greeted me at the door, but she didn't wag her tail. _____

5. Leonardo painted this picture.   _____

6. Grant offered Lee his hand, and they walked out   _____
   the door.

7. She gave me a tip because I helped her.   _____

8. My son, who has the measles, missed school.   _____

9. Pam and Cesar are leaving at noon.   _____

10. The night crew cleaned the office and emptied   _____
    the trash.

Compound-Complex Sentences

A **compound-complex sentence** is just what the name implies: it contains two or more independent clauses and at least one dependent clause.

DC   IC
While the storm raged outside, Bert completed his homework,

IC
and Elizabeth called her mother.

PRACTICE SET 8–5

Directions: Add dependent clauses to the following compound sentences to make them compound-complex.

Example: When _I go to a restaurant_ , I order dessert, but I never finish it.

1. My suitcase is packed, but I am not ready to leave because _____.

2. While _____, Andy parked the car, and Melissa bought the food.

3. Todd requested the song that _____, but I didn't know how to play it.

4. I didn't deserve the money, but since _____, I am going to spend it.

5. Unless _____, I will call your mother, and I will tell her what you said.

PRACTICE SET 8–6

Directions: Underline the verbs twice and the subjects once in all of the independent clauses in the following sentences.

Example: I knew why she was crying, but I did not apologize.

1. Margo ran through the open field, yet she never looked up at the sky.

2. Before we watch the Super Bowl, we always order pizza.

3. Dishes that contain homemade pasta are the specialty of this restaurant.

4. Parker and his brother work at the gas station.

5. When the coach fell, he sprained his ankle, so he went to the doctor.

6. We drove through several states, including Georgia, Alabama, Mississippi, Louisiana, and North Carolina.

7. They sold their house and moved to New York.

8. I ordered two appetizers, but the waiter brought me only one.

9. She does what she wants.

10. While we watched the parade, it started to rain, so we ran home.

Coordination and Subordination

The lessons in this chapter teach how to classify sentences according to structure. The important part of this lesson is not simply remembering the names of the various sentence types, but learning to use these different types of sentences to express your ideas in a concise, interesting way.

Compound sentences *coordinate* ideas, meaning that they express ideas that are about equal in importance:

I stood at attention, and I saluted the flag.

Complex sentences *subordinate* ideas, meaning that one idea is the major area of the sentence's focus while the other idea contributes some extra information— maybe why or when the major idea happened:

While I stood at attention, I saluted the flag.

You probably could express your ideas using all simple sentences, but as you learn to vary your sentences and include compound, complex, and compound-complex sentences, your writing style will improve. Examine the following simple sentences:

Lisa cleared the table.

Lisa washed the dishes.

Lisa did not clean the counter.

We could use coordination to combine the ideas like this:

Lisa cleared the table and washed the dishes, *but* she did not clean the counter.

Here is another example:

Franklin fell out of that tree. Franklin broke his arm.

We could use subordination to combine ideas, at the same time letting the reader see the importance of time in the two events:

Franklin broke his arm *when* he fell out of that tree.

TEST YOURSELF

Directions: Identify the following sentences as simple, compound, complex, or compound-complex.

1. We put on our raincoats and ran outside. _____

2. Before I answered her question, I scratched my head and cleared my throat. _____

3. You should never hang wind chimes that disturb the neighbors. _____

4. Winston Churchill faced many hardships, yet he never gave in to defeat. _____

5. I closed my eyes when I heard the crash, so I would not be a very good witness. _____

6. Chicken chow mein is made with chicken, onions, celery, and bean sprouts. _____

7. She couldn't see the board, nor could she hear what the professor was saying. _____

8. Camels, which have two humps, are often mistaken for dromedaries. _____

9. I don't know what you paid, but it was probably too much. _____

10. The cradle of civilization lay between the Tigris and the Euphrates rivers. _____

COMPOSITION WARM-UP

Directions: Combine the following simple sentences to make one compound, complex, or compound-complex sentence.

1. Luis enjoys watching football on television. He has never seen a live game in a stadium. _____

   _____

2. Tim took this picture of a beautiful sunrise. He developed the picture himself.

   _____

3. The department's holiday party was held last Saturday. I had the flu. I couldn't go. _____

4. Several fans wanted Elvis Presley's autograph after the concert. They stormed the stage. Elvis feared for his life. _____

   _____

5. Not all taxpayers can compute their own taxes. The laws are complicated. Some taxpayers must pay an accountant or tax service for help. _____

   _____

6. Snow and rain covered most of the West this morning. Travelers were stranded for hours. Several airports have now reopened. _____

   _____

7. Music companies have taken a strong position on copyright theft. They file suits against people who do not pay for downloads. _____

   _____

8. EBay is the world's largest shopping market. You can buy anything from a
   used book to a new car at a low price. _____

   _____

9. The best movies are released in December. People have time to see films
   during holiday vacations. Producers want their films to be eligible for the
   year's Academy Award nominations. _____

   _____

10. Americans like a lot of personal space. They don't like the people with whom
    they are speaking to stand too close. _____

    _____

COMPOSITION PRACTICE

Directions: Imagine that you have just won a million dollars.

(1) Write two **compound** sentences about what you would buy for yourself.
(2) Write two **complex** sentences about where you would travel.
(3) Write two **compound-complex** sentences about whom you would help.

WORD WATCHERS

Some words are misspelled so frequently that you may think the incorrect spelling is correct simply because you are used to seeing the words spelled that way. Listed below are some words that you should learn to spell correctly.

athlete   (not athelete) Tip: Pronounce it correctly—ATH lete.

congratulations (not congradulations) Tip: Don't confuse this with graDuation.

grammar   (not grammer) Tip: You'll get an *A* if you remember to spell grammar with an *a*.

mathematics   (not mathmatics) Tip: Look for *them* in mathematics.

writing   (not writting) Tip: Doubling the consonant *t* shortens the vowel *i*. *Writting* would rhyme with *sitting*.

a lot   (not alot) Tip: Always two words.

convenience   (not convience) Tip: Sound this one out to be sure you include each sound—con ven i ence.

WORD WATCHERS PRACTICE SET

Directions: Circle the word that is spelled *incorrectly* in each sentence.

1. The coach congradulated the athlete on beating the record time.

2. My mathematics class is much easier than my creative writting class.

3. You can't make alot of grammar mistakes if you want to receive a good grade on your paper.

4. Writing an outline should not be considered an inconvience.

5. A world-class athelete can excel in a lot of different sports.

Part 2

Handbook

Chapter 9

Sentence Fragments and Run-on Sentences

You have probably learned "the rules" about constructing sentences before. At some point in your study of English grammar, somebody undoubtedly taught you that a sentence is a "complete thought." If you had trouble understanding what that meant, you probably were not alone. Some grammatically correct sentences do not seem to express complete thoughts:

It is.

They did.

He might.

Any word grouping that makes an independent clause is a sentence. Complete thought or not, the examples above are sentences because they are independent clauses.

As you study this chapter, use the lessons you have already learned about phrases, clauses, and sentence construction to help you identify sentence fragments and run-on sentences.

Avoid sentence fragments.

A **sentence fragment** is an incomplete sentence—something is missing. Length is never a determiner of whether a grammatical construction is a sentence or a fragment. Both sentences and fragments can be long or short. A sentence is an independent clause containing a subject and a verb; it can stand by itself to express a complete thought. A fragment may have a subject and a verb, but it is not an independent clause and cannot stand alone as a sentence.

Sentence: It is late.

Fragment: Since it is late.

Sentence fragments can occur for many different reasons.

- **The subject may be missing.**

   Fragment: Went to the mall to buy a birthday gift.

   Sentence: *My friend* went to the mall to buy a birthday gift.

- **The verb or part of the verb phrase may be missing.**

   Fragment: The car sputtering and shaking at every red light.

   Sentence: The car *was* sputtering and shaking at every red light.

- **The independent clause may be missing.**

   Fragment: Because my favorite television show has been canceled.

   Sentence: Because my favorite television show has been canceled, *I am going to write a letter to the local NBC station.*

   Fragment: Feeling tired after a long day at the office.

   Sentence: *He was* feeling tired after a long day at the office.

PRACTICE SET 9–1

Directions: In the blanks at the right, label the following word groups as sentences or fragments.

Example: Until I find the prescription for my
allergy pills.   *fragment*

1. To prepare delicious barbecued ribs for the picnic.   _____

2. Her oldest sister and business partner.   _____

3. Who brought us the light fixtures we had ordered.   _____

4. The bear and her cubs climbing the trees by the creek.   _____

5. Professional sporting events usually start on time.   _____

There are several ways to correct sentence fragments.

You can add words.

This method works well when a basic sentence part, like the subject or the verb, is obviously missing.

Fragment: Quickly threw a blanket over the smoldering fire on the stove.

Sentence: *The babysitter* quickly threw a blanket over the smoldering fire on the stove.

Fragment: The truck broken down by the entrance ramp on the freeway.

Sentence: The truck *had* broken down by the entrance ramp on the freeway.

You can change or eliminate words.

Fragment: Although rain had been predicted for days.

Sentence: Rain had been predicted for days.

OR

Moreover, rain had been predicted for days.

Be sure to distinguish among subordinating conjunctions, transitional expressions, and conjunctive adverbs.

A subordinating conjunction introduces a dependent clause.

subordinating conjunction

Fragment: *Since*   he failed his driving test.

See Chapters 7 and 16 for lists of subordinating conjunctions.

A transitional expression introduces an independent clause.

transitional expression

Sentence: *In fact,*   he failed his driving test.

See Chapter 11 for a complete list of transitional expressions.

A conjunctive adverb introduces an independent clause.

conjunctive adverb

Sentence: *However,*   he failed his driving test.

See Chapter 16 for a list of conjunctive adverbs.

You can attach the fragment to the sentence that comes before or after it.

Fragment: The coach assigned the starting position to Carolyn. The fastest sprinter on the relay team.

Sentence: The coach assigned the starting position to Carolyn, the fastest sprinter on the relay team.

PRACTICE SET 9–2

Directions: Correct each of the following sentence fragments.

Example: As the captain attempted to turn the ship around.

As the captain attempted to turn the ship around, passengers rushed to the upper deck.

OR

The captain attempted to turn the ship around.

1. One of the advantages of traveling by train.

2. The police officer chasing the escaped fugitive.

3. When he moved from Atlanta to Houston.

4. Whom we met at the Buccaneers' opening game.

5. To create an impressive Thanksgiving dinner.

 **Quick Tip**

Be careful not to create sentence fragments when you use words and phrases like *for example, for instance, whereas, such as,* and *like*. If you begin a sentence with *such as*, you will automatically have a fragment.

Fragment: For example, my parents and my children.

Fragment: Whereas George's goals are rather unclear.

Fragment: Such as Florida and Texas.

Composition Clue

As you may have noticed, identifying isolated groups of words as fragments is much easier than finding fragments in your own writing. To solve this problem, you must learn to proofread effectively. The best way to proofread for sentence fragments is to read your writing very slowly aloud, stopping *emphatically* between sentences. In this way, you can *hear* the incomplete word groups.

If reading aloud is not possible, you should try to read very slowly to yourself, pronouncing each word carefully and concentrating on each sentence as a separate unit. Using this technique, you won't unconsciously connect word groups that you have actually punctuated as separate sentences. Another option is to read your work from the end to the beginning, one sentence at a time, so that you will be able to see your sentences out of context.

PRACTICE SET 9–3

Directions: Correct the fragments in the following paragraphs by adding words, changing or eliminating words, or attaching the fragments to make complete sentences.

Most people who have lived or traveled in the southern United States are familiar with kudzu. The leafy green vine that covers trees, drapes over shrubbery, and engulfs entire landscapes. Kudzu, described as "the vine that ate the South," imported from Asia one hundred years ago to beautify the landscape and prevent soil erosion. Since 1970, however, it has been considered a weed and a harmful one at that.

Like kudzu, invasive weeds running rampant across the North American continent. They are responsible for the decline of innumerable plant and animal species. Which are either threatened or endangered by extinction. According to a recent study. These weeds follow only habitat destruction as a leading danger to the world's ecology. The Interior Department claims that invasive weeds infest more than 100 million acres in the United States. The damage caused to agriculture, rangeland, and recreational areas amounting to billions of dollars annually.

While environmental problems, such as chemical pollution or hazardous waste, can be cleaned up or may disappear with time. Weeds present a more difficult dilemma. Biological invasions reproduce themselves and can last forever. What has caused this colossal environmental problem? The answer is that we live in a much smaller world than ever before. Today, global travel and trade enable invasive weeds to move easily from one continent or ecosystem to another. Sometimes intentionally, sometimes not.

One of the major difficulties involved in solving this ecological problem is that the weeds cross so many boundary lines. It is not a situation that governments designed to handle. Nevertheless, numerous local, state, and federal agencies involved in the crusade against invasive weeds. Before he left office in 2001, President Clinton ordered the creation of a National Invasive Species Council and increased funding to solve the problem. Although this step may not be much more effective than pulling a few weeds in an entire lawnful. It is important in alerting Americans to the threat. Since spraying and weeding are solutions which create problems of their own. Perhaps early detection and prevention are our only hope.

Composition Clue

Occasionally, sentence fragments are acceptable:

For emphasis: Not a day passes without tears. *Not a day!*

To answer a question: Will the president run for a second term? *Absolutely.*

Dialogue: "I'm waiting patiently for the weather to cool off." "Me, too."

In formal writing, however, you should avoid using sentence fragments. Most grammarians view fragments as errors.

Avoid run-on sentences.

Run-on sentences have various names: run-ons, blended sentences, run-togethers, fused sentences, comma splices. The name doesn't really matter. All of these labels refer to the same error—the incorrect joining of independent clauses.

Run-on sentences are not necessarily long. Even short independent clauses strung together create a run-on.

Run-on: Kenny loves photography he bought a digital camera.

Run-on: Kenny loves photography, he bought a digital camera.

These two sentences are faulty because two independent clauses are joined incorrectly.

Correct: Kenny loves photography, so he bought a digital camera.

There are four simple ways to correct run-on sentences.

Create separate sentences.

Divide independent clauses into separate sentences, using a capital letter and appropriate end punctuation.

Run-on: Our aging cat has diabetes we have to give him an insulin shot daily.

Correct: Our aging cat has diabetes. We have to give him an insulin shot daily.

This method works well if the independent clauses are long or are of different sentence types and need different end punctuation.

Run-on: Many Americans lack medical insurance, where can they go for help?

Correct: Many Americans lack medical insurance. Where can they go for help?

PRACTICE SET 9–4

Directions: Correct the following run-ons by dividing them into separate sentences.

Example: I can't balance my checkbook will you help me find my mistakes?

I can't balance my checkbook. Will you help me find my mistakes?

1. Most Americans own televisions, vacuum cleaners, and microwave ovens cell phones and computers are becoming commonplace as well.

2. The Biltmore House in Asheville, North Carolina, is a major tourist attraction it includes gardens and a dairy as well as the mansion itself.

3. Signing up early for college classes is important students can get the courses they want and avoid long registration lines.

4. Forest fires raging out of control endanger lives and property fighting these fires costs millions of taxpayer dollars each year.

5. Pinecones are popular holiday decorations they are attractive, long-lasting, and unbreakable.

Coordinate the sentences.

Join the two independent clauses with a comma and a coordinating conjunction (*and, but, or, nor, for, yet, so*). This method is effective if the clauses are closely related and fairly short.

Run-on: The grass grows rapidly in the summer we mow it weekly.

Correct: The grass grows rapidly in the summer, *so* we mow it weekly.

Run-on: My car is brand-new it is always in the repair shop.

Correct: My car is brand-new, *but* it is always in the repair shop.

Composition Clue

Be sure to choose the coordinating conjunction that shows the relationship between the ideas most clearly.

Conjunction	Meaning
and	indicates an addition
but	indicates a contrast
yet	indicates a contrast
or	indicates a choice
for	indicates a reason
nor	indicates a negative choice
so	indicates a result

PRACTICE SET 9–5

Directions: Correct the following run-ons by adding a comma and a coordinating conjunction (*and*, *but*, *or*, *nor*, *for*, *yet*, *so*) to each sentence. Make sure to choose the conjunction that most clearly shows the relationship between the ideas.

Example: Mr. Wilson mowed his lawn he edged the sidewalk and the flower beds.

Mr. Wilson mowed his lawn, and he edged the sidewalk and the flower beds.

1. Orchids are beautiful flowers growing them is quite time-consuming.

2. Angie has renewed her subscription to *Time* magazine she enjoys reading about politics and current issues.

3. Our refrigerator is almost empty we need to go grocery shopping.

4. Susan and Michael can see a movie tonight they can go out to dinner with their friends.

5. Martin has a high grade point average he is an outstanding baseball player.

Use a semicolon.

Using a semicolon (;) is an effective way to join fairly short and closely related independent clauses. (See Chapter 11 for more information on semicolons.) Remember that a semicolon separates independent clauses; a complete sentence must stand on each side. However, the clause following the semicolon does not begin with a capital letter.

Run-on: The boat has finally been repaired, we can go water-skiing next weekend.

Correct: The boat has finally been repaired; we can go water-skiing next weekend.

Often, semicolons are followed by conjunctive adverbs or transitional expressions. These linking words or phrases emphasize the relationship between the two independent clauses.

The boat has finally been repaired; *therefore*, we can go water-skiing next weekend.

Note that a semicolon precedes the transition *therefore* and a comma follows it. Be careful, though. If a transition comes in the middle of one independent clause, you can't use a semicolon; you must use two commas.

The repair costs, *however*, were extremely high.

PRACTICE SET 9–6

Directions: Use semicolons to correct the following run-on sentences. If a sentence is already correct, write "correct" in the margin.

Example: Most children watch too much television, often, the TV functions as a babysitter.

Most children watch too much television; often, the TV functions as a babysitter.

1. The sunset, however, has never been more spectacular.

2. Jake concentrates on taking notes in class, therefore, he has little trouble when studying for a test.

3. Flannery O'Connor's short stories are set in the South, they contain unusual characters and unexpected violence.

4. One candidate was concerned about health care and education reform, his opponent worried about the economy and international politics.

5. Organ transplants have become very successful, however, there are many more patients waiting for surgery than there are organ donors.

Make one of the independent clauses into a dependent clause.

Another effective way to join independent clauses and avoid run-on sentences is to change one of the independent clauses into a dependent clause. To make this change, you must add a subordinating conjunction to create an adverb clause or a relative pronoun, like *who, which, that,* to create an adjective clause. (For the punctuation of dependent clauses, see Chapter 10; for more information on relative pronouns, see Chapter 16.)

Run-on: Juvenile obesity is a major cause of physical and emotional illness, parents must address this problem.

subordinating conjunction

Correct: *Because*   *juvenile obesity is a major cause of physical and emotional illness*, parents must address this problem. (adverb clause)

relative pronoun

Correct: Parents must address the problem of juvenile obesity,   *which*   *is a major cause of physical and emotional illness.* (adjective clause)

Be careful about the adverb *then*. Although it looks like a subordinating conjunction, it is not. You are likely to create a run-on if a clause beginning with *then* is not written properly as an independent sentence.

Run-on: I washed the dishes, then I settled down to watch my favorite TV show.

Correct: I washed the dishes. Then I settled down to watch my favorite TV show.

Correct: I washed the dishes, and then I settled down to watch my favorite TV show.

Correct: I washed the dishes; then I settled down to watch my favorite TV show.

PRACTICE SET 9–7

Directions: Correct the following run-on sentences by turning one independent clause into a dependent clause. In this exercise, add subordinating conjunctions to create adverb clauses or relative pronouns to create adjective clauses.

Example: Termites cause serious problems for homeowners these pests have become resistant to many pesticides.

Because termites have become resistant to many pesticides, they cause serious problems for homeowners.

OR

Termites, which cause serious problems for homeowners, have become resistant to many pesticides.

1. Princess Diana died in an automobile accident in Paris in 1997 she is still mourned by millions of people worldwide.

2. Joseph forgot to pay his utility bill the electric company turned off his power.

3. Peggy Smith is a very successful realtor, she is sincere, honest, and hard-working.

4. The antique cabinet was badly damaged in the move a restoration expert should appraise it.

5. School uniforms have positive effects on students many public schools now require them.

Composition Clue

Although the four methods above are the primary ways to correct run-on sentences, any technique that combines ideas without joining independent clauses improperly will work. Consider reworking a sentence, changing the word order, adding words, or eliminating words without changing the meaning. The solution depends on the particular word groups involved.

Run-on: Teaching children to dance improves their coordination it also gives them self-confidence.

Correct: Teaching children to dance *improves* their coordination *and gives* them self-confidence. (compound verb)

Run-on: Miss Kissinger was my high school French teacher, she sparked my desire to visit Paris.

Correct: Miss Kissinger, *my high school French teacher,* sparked my desire to visit Paris. (appositive)

Run-on: Otis sped down the highway, he barely avoided a collision with a slow-moving tractor.

Correct: *Speeding down the highway,* Otis barely avoided a collision with a slow-moving tractor. (verbal phrase)

PRACTICE SET 9–8

Directions: Correct the following run-on sentences. In this exercise, vary the correction methods, using each method at least once. Remember that you can change words, eliminate words, add words, or change word order. If a sentence is correct, write "correct" in the margin.

Examples:
You must proofread carefully for sentence errors, grammar mistakes weaken your writing.

You must proofread carefully for sentence errors. Grammar mistakes weaken your writing.

OR

Grammar mistakes weaken your writing, so you must proofread carefully for sentence errors.

OR

You must proofread carefully for sentence errors; grammar mistakes weaken your writing.

OR

You must proofread carefully for sentence errors because grammar mistakes weaken your writing.

OR

You must proofread carefully for grammar mistakes that weaken your writing.

1. Some states require motorcyclists to wear helmets, others do not.

2. Depression is common in elderly people it can be treated effectively with medication.

3. Hurricanes pose a threat to homeowners in coastal areas these storms can destroy a house in a very short period of time.

4. Camping is a good family activity that fosters cooperation and creativity.

5. Drought conditions have existed for months, however, people get annoyed if rain ruins their weekend plans.

PRACTICE SET 9–9

Directions: Correct the run-on sentences in the following paragraphs by using a variety of the methods discussed in this chapter.

As a response to danger, stress enables a human being to channel physical resources of strength and speed for protection. A certain amount of stress is, therefore, necessary for survival, but chronic stress—stress experienced over a long period of time—weakens the body physically and mentally. Emotional stress can weaken the immune system, it increases the chances of coronary disease and viral infection. Stress can even affect one's body shape the chemical reactions connected to the stress response may cause fat cells to accumulate in the abdomen.

Not everyone responds in the same way to particular stressors, for example, there are significant gender differences. Although women's blood pressure appears to be less affected by stress than men's, women react to a greater range of stressors and feel stress more often. Events of early childhood also influence how adults handle stress, children in unstable homes exhibit stronger reactions to adult stresses than do children raised in stable, supportive environments. Unfortunately, childhood stress seems to be an ever-increasing aspect of modern life.

Since totally eliminating stress from our lives is impossible, we must learn to handle it effectively. We can try to develop more stress-resistant behaviors. People who cope well with stressful situations tend to concentrate on immediate problems rather than on long-range ones, they are able to rationalize their troubles in a positive way, they have an optimistic outlook toward life and themselves. Meditation and other relaxation techniques, massage, exercise, and a strong support system also help to relieve stress. Finally, expressing our emotions—whether aloud to others or in written form—will contribute to a more functional, relaxed, stress-free life.

TEST YOURSELF

Directions: Label the following word groups as fragments (*F*), run-on sentences (*RS*), or correct sentences (*C*).

1. Whereas the cost of the rental car was very high.

2. Which she found at the bottom of her aunt's old cedar chest.

3. DNA evidence is commonly admitted in courtrooms in the United States.

4. The laurel tree is losing its leaves it must need water.

5. The tires that he recommends for my truck.

6. The triathlete rode his bike for an hour then he ran five miles.

7. The operating team having done everything they could to save the patient.

8. Cats are popular pets for people who live in apartments.

9. The milk spoiled the refrigerator was not cold enough.

10. Although we were sorry to miss the retirement party.

COMPOSITION WARM-UP

Directions: The following paragraphs contain fragments and run-on sentences. Correct them by changing punctuation and capitalization. You do *not* need to add, change, or delete words.

One of the most intriguing figures of the Civil War was Major General George McClellan. A graduate of West Point. McClellan suffered from an inflated ego and an inability to take action. So much so that some even accused him of cowardice. When McClellan took command of the Army of the Potomac, the recruits were a ragtag bunch of farmers. Who were inexperienced in the ways of war. He was an outstanding leader, organizing the troops and turning them into confident soldiers, however, he frequently showed a lack of respect for Lincoln, his commander-in-chief. He was nicknamed "The Young Napoleon." Not only for his leadership skills, but for his conceited and arrogant behavior.

McClellan's abilities did not extend to the battlefield, however. Often incorrectly convinced that his troops were vastly outnumbered and unwilling to put them in harm's way. He angered Lincoln by his refusal to engage the Army of the Potomac in battle. Or to push forward when they were close to victory. Lincoln's frustration showed in a famous letter he once wrote to McClellan. The letter, addressed to "My Dear McClellan," said, "If you are not using the army, I should like to borrow it for a short while," it was signed, "Yours respectfully, Abraham Lincoln." Lincoln finally relieved McClellan of his command in 1862, nevertheless, Lincoln had to tangle with him again when McClellan became the Democratic Party candidate for president in the 1864 election.

COMPOSITION PRACTICE

1. Write a sentence beginning with *although.*

2. Write a sentence containing the phrase *such as.*

3. Write two independent clauses joined by a semicolon.

4. Write two independent clauses joined by *however* and the appropriate punctuation.

5. Write two related sentences, starting the second one with *then.*

WORD WATCHERS

Some words are misspelled so frequently that you may think the incorrect spelling is correct simply because you are used to seeing the words spelled that way. Listed below are some words that you should learn to spell correctly.

develop   (not develop**e**) Tip: Adding the *e* on the end lengthens the *o* vowel. Develop**e** would rhyme with cantelope and envelope.

judgment   (not judgement) Tip: Some dictionaries list *judgement* with an *e* as an acceptable secondary spelling, but that spelling is really the British spelling. If you are not using other British spellings (like colour and honour) in your writing, you should not use this one either.

license   (not lisence) Tip: *C* before *s* in the alphabet.

occasion   (not occassion) Tip: Two *c*'s, one *s*.

separate   (not seperate) Tip: Keep your spelling skills up to **par** when you spell se**par**ate.

definitely   (not definately) Tip: Pronounce it correctly. There is an "it" in *definitely.*

(*continued*)

WORD WATCHERS PRACTICE SET

Directions: Circle the word or words that are spelled *incorrectly* in each sentence.

1. You must develop good judgement if you are going to have a driver's license.

2. I am definately going to separate my white clothes from my colored ones the next time I do the laundry.

3. On this special occasion, I will take poetic lisence and wish you all the joy your heart can hold.

4. It is my judgment that this is an appropriate occassion to have a little wine.

5. I do not want to develope a crush on Maurice, even though he and Felicity have gone their seperate ways.

Chapter 10

Commas

Commas separate, combine, emphasize, and clarify. Most writers, even skilled ones, have comma questions. However, comma usage can become less confusing if you follow three important guidelines:

1. Use a comma only when there is a grammatical reason to use it.
2. Do not overuse commas. Inserting a comma where it does not belong is just as wrong as omitting a comma where it does belong.
3. Learn the comma rules, apply them, and save the exceptions for later. Following the rules consistently will make you right most of the time.

Understanding basic sentence structure (see Chapters 1–8) simplifies comma usage. Students sometimes insert commas where there are pauses in oral reading or where "it sounds right." These practices often cause comma errors. It is best to follow the specific comma rules.

Use a comma before a coordinating conjunction that separates independent clauses.

Coordination occurs when a comma and a coordinating conjunction join two or more independent clauses. The coordinating conjunctions are *and, but, or, for, nor, so, yet.* You can use the mnemonic FANBOYS to help you remember this list:

For

And

Nor

But

Or

Yet

So

Since every independent clause has a subject and a verb, a subject/verb must appear on each side of the coordinating conjunction.

Remember that words can function as more than one part of speech.

For is a coordinating conjunction only if it means *because*; otherwise, it is a preposition.

Coordinating conjunction: I left, *for* the meeting was over.

Preposition: I left *for* the meeting.

But is usually a conjunction, but it can be a preposition if it means *except*, as in the following example:

Everyone *but* me got a new hat.

Use this formula to help you remember where to place the coordinating conjunction.

Independent clause**,**   coordinating conjunction   independent clause.

independent clause	coordinating conjunction	independent clause
We left for the airport two hours early**,**	but	we still missed our flight.

This sentence fits the coordination formula, so use a comma before the conjunction.

verb	coordinating conjunction	verb
We left for the airport two hours early	but	still missed our flight.

This sentence does not fit the coordination formula. The sentence simply has a compound verb, so no comma is needed.

If a coordinating conjunction joins two subordinate clauses, do not use a comma.

Alice said *that I should meet her at two o'clock* and *(that) we could drive to the party together.*

These are two noun clauses, not independent clauses. The word *that* tells you that the clauses are dependent, not independent.

The most effectively coordinated sentences are relatively short and closely related in meaning.

Ineffective coordination: I am a college freshman, and my girlfriend is from Indiana.

Effective coordination: I am a college freshman, and I want to major in elementary education.

PRACTICE SET 10–1

Directions: In the following sentences, add commas where needed. Write "correct" next to sentences that need no commas.

Example: He volunteered to work at the park, and he picked up garbage for two hours.

1. Gordon packs quickly and efficiently for his job requires frequent traveling.

2. Habit often determines where people shop and what they buy.

3. Christi will work out at the gym today or she will ride her bicycle for an hour.

4. My mother prepared everything ahead but the appetizers and the salad.

5. Shaina loves reading so she belongs to several book clubs.

6. The British enjoy warm scones and fresh cream at teatime.

7. Neither the producer nor the director wanted to shorten the film.

8. Ben does not enjoy playing golf nor does he like watching it on television.

9. The physical therapist thought that the patient was getting stronger and that he would soon be able to walk without crutches.

10. The athletes are exhausted yet they have no time to rest before the second practice session begins.

Use commas to separate items in a series.

A **series** is a list. If more than two items appear in a list, put commas between the items and before the conjunction. These items may consist of single words, phrases, or clauses.

A series of nouns: We served *chicken, rice,* and *asparagus* at the wedding.

A series of prepositional phrases: The defense attorney mailed the documents *to her client, to the prosecutor,* and *to the judge.*

A series of clauses: Parents usually care about *what their teenagers do, where they go,* and *how much money they spend.*

Quick Tip

Sometimes, for emphasis, the conjunction appears between every item in the series. In this case, do not use any commas.

The villain was irrational and greedy and cruel.

PRACTICE SET 10–2

Directions: In the following sentences, add commas where needed. Write "correct" next to sentences that need no commas.

Example: We pulled weeds, watered the flowers, and cut the grass.

1. The chef prepared the pasta with salmon peas and a creamy cheese sauce.

2. We went to the movies in Hyde Park ate dinner on Harbour Island and listened to jazz at a club in Ybor City.

3. World Cup ski races are held in Aspen and Vail and Beaver Creek.

4. The camping store sells jackets that repel water tents that fold easily and stoves that run on battery power.

5. The frustrated golfer hit balls into the lake into the sandtrap and into the nearby woods.

Use a comma to separate coordinate adjectives.

Coordinate adjectives are equal adjectives that modify the same noun. If adjectives are coordinate, place a comma between them. In order to decide if adjectives are coordinate, you must apply two tests:

1. Coordinate adjectives can be reversed and still make sense.
2. Coordinate adjectives can have an *and* between them and still make sense.

If both tests work well, the adjectives are coordinate, and you use a comma between them. If both tests don't work well, assume that the adjectives are not coordinate, and omit the comma.

He lives in an *old, dilapidated* house. (a dilapidated, old house; an old and dilapidated house—both of these phrases make sense. The adjectives are coordinate, so you use a comma between them.)

The *famous plastic* surgeon operates on Hollywood celebrities. (the plastic famous surgeon, the famous and plastic surgeon—neither of these phrases makes sense. The adjectives are not coordinate, so you do not use a comma.)

PRACTICE SET 10–3

Directions: In the following sentences, add commas where needed. Write "correct" next to sentences that need no commas.

Example: The sly, greedy fox attacked the chickens.

1. The sad disillusioned student considered withdrawing from college.

2. The tall distinguished gentleman in the front row of the auditorium is a successful software manufacturer.

3. Three copper pots are hanging over the stove in the kitchen.

4. The famous actor bought a bright red Porsche convertible.

5. The dark depressing film was based on a disastrous Antarctic expedition.

Use a comma after an introductory element.

An **introductory element** is a grammatical construction that appears at the beginning of a sentence. Many types of phrases and clauses introduce sentences and are followed by commas.

Use a comma after an introductory prepositional phrase.

A prepositional phrase at the beginning of a sentence takes a comma.

After the game, we hurried to the movie.

Because of his positive attitude and extensive product knowledge, the salesman earned high commissions.

(This long prepositional phrase begins with a prepositional expression, *because of*, and has a compound object, *attitude and knowledge*.)

If a sentence begins with more than one prepositional phrase, a comma should follow the last one.

prepositional phrase	prepositional phrase	prepositional phrase	
In the middle	*of the professor's lecture*	*on commas,*	the student fell asleep.

(This sentence begins with three prepositional phrases.)

Quick Tip

Some writers omit the comma after an introductory prepositional phrase if the phrase is very short.

At noon we take a lunch break.

OR

At noon, we take a lunch break.

Use a comma after an introductory adverb clause.

If an adverb clause comes at the beginning of a sentence, put a comma after it. If the adverb clause comes at the end of the sentence and follows the independent clause, do not use a comma.

introductory adverb clause
Because we had overslept, we rushed to get to work.

(This introductory adverb clause is followed by a comma.)

adverb clause
We rushed to get to work *because we had overslept.*

(This adverb clause follows the independent clause and takes no comma.)

Use a comma after a verbal phrase that is not the subject of the sentence.

Since participles are adjectives and can never be the subjects of sentences, a participial phrase at the beginning of a sentence is always followed by a comma. With introductory gerund and infinitive phrases, comma use varies. If the gerund or infinitive phrase is the subject of the sentence, no comma follows it. If the gerund or infinitive phrase is not the subject, a comma follows it.

participial phrase
Coming home late from the party, Janet had a flat tire.

(A comma follows the introductory participial phrase.)

gerund phrase
Coming home late from the party created a problem for Janet.

(No comma follows the gerund phrase used as a subject.)

infinitive phrase
To understand commas well, you must study hard.

(A comma follows the introductory infinitive phrase.)

infinitive phrase
To understand commas well is crucial for good writers.

(No comma follows the infinitive phrase used as the subject.)

Use a comma after a transitional word or phrase at the beginning of a sentence.

A **transition** is a word or phrase that shows the relationship between two sentences or paragraphs. Various kinds of transitions show various kinds of relationships. For example, some transitions show cause and effect (*thus, therefore, as a result, consequently*), and others show time (*first, second, next, finally*). If a single word or a short prepositional phrase is transitional and comes at the beginning of a sentence, a comma should follow it. (See Chapter 11 for a comprehensive list of transitional expressions.)

Therefore, John got a job at an advertising agency.

In fact, he was hired after only one short interview.

Use a comma after a mild interjection.

An **interjection** is a word that expresses feeling or emotion and plays no grammatical role in the sentence. If the expression of feeling is strong, an exclamation point follows it. However, a mild interjection at the beginning of a sentence takes a comma. This rule applies also to the words *yes* and *no* when they are interjections.

Oh, that's nice.

Yes, I would like some ice cream with my birthday cake.

Ouch! You're really hurting me.

PRACTICE SET 10–4

Directions: In the following sentences, add commas where needed. Write "correct" next to sentences that need no commas.

Example: After the next song, you will hear a famous duet.

1. If you enjoy the drama of athletics you probably watch the Olympics on television.

2. Yes I will help you with your essay during my office hours on Tuesday.

3. Staring sadly out of the bus window Ralph watched his hometown disappear in the distance.

4. After climbing for several days the hiking party finally reached the summit of the mountain.

5. On the other hand the meeting will probably be canceled.

6. The telephone had stopped ringing before Abby was able to answer it.

7. At the beginning of the ninth inning the score was tied.

8. To write an effective essay is not an easy task.

9. We bought our movie tickets online because we didn't want to wait at the theater.

10. To prepare your income tax return you should see a qualified accountant.

Restrictive and nonrestrictive clauses and phrases require careful consideration.

Don't be intimidated by the terms *restrictive* and *nonrestrictive*. *Restrictive* simply means "essential," and *nonrestrictive* means "nonessential." When deciding whether to use commas, you must determine how important a clause or phrase is to the meaning—not the structure—of the sentence. This rule applies to adjective clauses and participial phrases, and it is one of the most difficult rules for writers to understand. Specific grammar rules dictate most comma placement; however, this comma rule requires a decision.

Ask yourself: Is the modifying clause or phrase needed to tell something essential about a noun and make the meaning of the sentence clear? If an adjective clause or phrase identifies a noun and makes the meaning of a sentence clear, it is **restrictive,** or essential, and does not require commas. Examine this sentence:

A woman *who is the director of a company* earns a high salary.

Who is the director of a company is an adjective clause. If you leave it out, you still have a structurally complete sentence: *A woman ~~who is the director of a company~~ earns a high salary.* However, the meaning of the sentence is not clear. You need the clause to tell *which* woman. Since the clause is essential to the meaning, don't separate it from the sentence with commas.

On the other hand, if the adjective clause or phrase simply gives extra, added information and is not essential to make the meaning of the sentence clear, it is **nonrestrictive,** or nonessential, and you set it off with commas.

Maria Ortiz, *who is the director of a company,* earns a high salary.

Who is the director of a company is an adjective clause, but if you leave it out, your reader still knows whom you are talking about, Maria Ortiz.

Maria Ortiz~~, who is the director of a company,~~ earns a high salary.

The clause is not needed to identify, so you set it off with commas.
Now compare these two sentences:

The city *where he went to college* is in Georgia.

The adjective clause *where he went to college* is essential to identify the city and make the meaning of the sentence clear. Therefore, you do not set it off with commas.

Atlanta, *where he went to college,* is in Georgia.

The adjective clause *where he went to college* is added, nonessential information, so you set it off with commas.

Some additional hints will help you decide if a clause is restrictive or nonrestrictive.

1. Usually, clauses or phrases that modify proper nouns are nonrestrictive and take commas. Because the specific names appear, you do not need the clause or phrase to identify the nouns.

   Hillsborough Community College, *which is located in Tampa,* has four campuses.

2. Clauses or phrases beginning with the relative pronoun *that* are always restrictive; therefore, they never require commas.

   The suit *that he bought for the conference* was very expensive.

With restrictives and nonrestrictives, comma usage is usually an all-or-nothing proposition. Use either two commas or none.

Incorrect: Mark Twain, who wrote *Huckleberry Finn* traveled extensively in Egypt.

Correct: Mark Twain, who wrote *Huckleberry Finn*, traveled extensively in Egypt.

Incorrect: The raccoon, that sneaked into the garage was frightened.

Correct: The raccoon that sneaked into the garage was frightened.

One comma will set off a nonrestrictive clause or phrase only when the clause or phrase comes at the end of the sentence.

Tonight we are going to see *Cabaret*, which is a play set in Germany before World War II.

Appositive words and phrases (see Chapter 4) are also restrictive or nonrestrictive. Remember that an appositive is a noun that follows another noun and renames it. Most appositive phrases are nonrestrictive and are set off by commas. However, if the phrase is very short, closely related to the noun, or essential to meaning, consider it restrictive and do not use commas.

Billy Crystal, *the director of the play*, is a famous actor and comedian.

I enjoyed reading *A Tale of Two Cities*, *a novel by Charles Dickens*.

The novel *A Tale of Two Cities* is set during the French Revolution.

My son *Adam* is an investment banker on Wall Street.

In the last two examples, the appositives identify the nouns they rename, so they do not take commas.

PRACTICE SET 10–5

Directions: In the following sentences, add commas where needed. Write "correct" next to sentences that need no commas.

Example: My Uncle Mike, who speaks Spanish, is going to work in Mexico.

1. John Fitzgerald Kennedy the thirty-fifth president of the United States was assassinated in 1963.

2. The vandals who destroyed the computer lab were caught the next day.

3. Denzel Washington whose movies range from action thrillers to serious drama is a versatile performer.

4. The story "The Most Dangerous Game" is set on a fictitious island in the Caribbean Sea.

5. Most people celebrated the end of the twentieth century in the year 2000 which was not really the end of the millennium.

6. Colleges that offer a flexible course schedule usually attract nontraditional students.

7. My neighbors moved to Black Mountain a small town in North Carolina.

8. *Fences* which was written by August Wilson is a play about barriers of all kinds.

9. This sculpture is one which they purchased at a local art show.

10. Vijay and Murti lived in the city where the earthquake occurred.

Use commas to set off interrupting expressions.

Interrupting expressions are words and phrases that are not part of the main idea of the sentence. They are always set off by commas, and they can appear at the beginning, the middle, or the end of a sentence. Several types of expressions are interrupters.

Use commas to set off parenthetical expressions.

Parenthetical expressions are true interrupters, for they are comments (words or phrases) "stuck" into the middle of a sentence.

The dishonest employee is, *I am sure*, not working there anymore.

You are in trouble, *I think*, because of your irrational behavior.

Use commas to set off transitions.

Transitions are words or phrases that show the relationship between two sentences or paragraphs. If a transition comes at the beginning of a sentence, it is an introductory element, and you must follow it with a comma. If it comes in the middle of an independent clause, set it off with commas. If it comes at the end of a sentence, put a comma before it.

However, the judge is an extremely impatient individual.

The judge, *however*, is an extremely impatient individual.

The judge is an extremely impatient individual, *however*.

Use commas to set off nouns of direct address.

Direct address is speech directed to a person, using his or her name or title. A noun of direct address never has a grammatical function in the sentence, such as subject or object. A noun of direct address can come at the beginning, middle, or end of the sentence.

Sam, please open the door.

I do not know, *Mother*, if I can meet you at the mall today.

Here is my assignment, *Professor Curtis*.

Use commas to set off echo questions.

Echo questions echo declarative statements and turn them into questions. Sometimes called **tag questions,** echo questions come in the middle or at the end of a sentence.

Next week is spring break, *isn't it?*

If the echo question comes in the middle of the sentence, set it off with commas.

You're coming with me, *aren't you,* when I leave for the hospital?

Use commas to separate expressions of negative contrast.

Expressions of negative contrast always involve a negative word, like *not* or *unlike*, and two different ideas. Sometimes these constructions are called **contradictory phrases** or **contrasted elements.** A negative contrast can come in the middle or at the end of a sentence and will require one or two commas, depending on its location.

Mr. Stein's daughter is moving to New York, *not Chicago.*

An ophthalmologist, *never an optician*, can prescribe medication.

PRACTICE SET 10–6

Directions: In the following sentences, add commas where needed.

Example: You know, of course, that the rebate deadline has expired.

1. The professor never the teaching assistant turns in the final grades.

2. Congressman Davis is it true that you are planning to run for governor?

3. They are considering a trip to Peru not Puerto Rico.

4. This medication according to recent laboratory studies may have severe side effects.

5. The roses should be pruned however before you fertilize them.

6. Be sure to call me Sarah if you are going to be late for your appointment.

7. The arts and crafts festival was really fun wasn't it?

8. This trial has been I truly believe a mockery of justice.

9. Do not open the test booklet until the buzzer sounds students.

10. I ordered a sandwich and potato chips not soup and a salad.

Use commas to set off absolute constructions.

An **absolute construction** is a phrase consisting of a noun plus a participle or participial phrase. The absolute construction adds meaning to a sentence without specifically connecting to any sentence part. The entire phrase is a unit and may appear anywhere in a sentence. If the absolute construction appears at the beginning of a sentence, use a comma after it; if it appears at the end of a sentence, put a comma before it; if it appears in the middle of the sentence, set it off with commas.

Her long hair blowing in the breeze, the young girl looked like a model.

The teenager left for the game, *his poor test grade quickly forgotten.*

The kitten, *its head buried in its blanket*, was sound asleep.

Use commas to set off direct quotations.

Direct quotations repeat someone's exact words. Use a comma after words, such as *said*, *stated*, or *exclaimed*, that announce a direct quotation.

His father said, "I am very proud of your performance in the game."

When the quotation appears before the announcing words, use a comma after the quotation unless it is a question or exclamation. Question marks and exclamation points take the place of commas.

"I am having a bad day," the child whimpered to her grandfather.

"What is wrong with the video recorder?" the producer asked.

When the announcing words interrupt a one-sentence quotation, set them off with commas.

"My husband has not felt well," the woman told the doctor, "since we returned from our cruise."

When the quotation consists of more than one sentence, be sure to use a period between the sentences. Otherwise, you will create a run-on sentence.

Incorrect: "Let's go home now," Helen said, "I am getting very tired."

Correct: "Let's go home now," Helen said. "I am getting very tired."

Remember that commas and periods always go inside quotation marks; other marks, such as semicolons, colons, question marks, exclamation points, vary according to the particular situation. See Chapter 11 to learn more about punctuating quotations.

Be careful about confusing direct quotations with indirect quotations. An indirect quotation repeats what someone has said but paraphrases it. Indirect quotations do not require quotation marks or commas.

Indirect quotation: Arthur's professor said that she would give him an extension on the paper.

Direct quotation: Arthur's professor said, "I will give you an extension on the paper."

PRACTICE SET 10–7

Directions: In the following sentences, add commas where needed. Write "correct" next to sentences that need no commas.

Example: "Pay at the door," said the usher.

1. "I can't finish this chapter" Grace complained.

2. My daughter says that she wants to leave early on Monday morning.

3. I was unable to cash my check the bank having closed for Presidents' Day.

4. "What do you think of this fabric?" the designer asked her client.

5. Her eyes shining with happiness the bride walked slowly down the church aisle.

6. "We can leave" Aaron whispered "before the game is over."

7. The football player his uniform caked with mud felt frustrated and angry over the penalty.

8. The professor warned "Make sure to study your notes for the grammar test."

9. "Watch out!" the crane operator yelled to the pedestrians below.

10. "The movie starts at five o'clock" he reported. "I'll meet you in the lobby."

Use commas when appropriate for dates and addresses, names and titles, informal salutations, large numbers, and statistics.

Place commas correctly in dates and addresses.

Dates and addresses having two or more parts take commas *between* and *after* the parts.

I was born on Monday, March 29, 1943, in Ohio.

Note these important exceptions. Do *not* put commas between the following:

Month/Day:	June 3 is my birthday.
Month/Year:	He graduated in June 2006.
Day/Month/Year:	Our last day of school was 3 June 2006.
Number/Street:	We lived at 510 Lake Avenue.
State/Zip Code:	They sent money to a post office box in Atlanta, Georgia 30338.

On Monday, June 12, 1994, the young attorney opened his first office at 600 Jackson Street, Suite 200, Tampa, Florida 33602, and began practicing criminal law.

Place commas correctly in names and titles.

If a title or an abbreviation follows a name in a sentence, put commas *between* the name and title and *after* the title.

I met Joseph Bartlett, M.D., at the conference on infectious diseases.

Dr. Martin Luther King, Jr., was deeply inspired by the teachings of Mohandas Gandhi.

Place a comma after a salutation in a letter.

A comma follows the salutation in an informal letter.

Dear Santa,

Place commas correctly in numbers and statistics.

It is common practice to place commas within numbers over three digits to make them more readable. Start at the right, and place a comma after every third digit.

The bankrupt business was liquidating over 3,500,000 novelty items at vastly reduced prices.

 *Quick Tip*

With easy-to-read numbers of four digits, a comma is usually optional.

The club members sold 2500 boxes of cookies.

Also, certain large numbers never take commas: social security numbers, telephone numbers, driver's license and credit card numbers, and long addresses.

98430 Fletcher Avenue

In any case, consistency in the handling of numbers is important. See Chapter 11 for more on writing numbers.

Commas separate certain kinds of information and statistics. Note the following examples:

five feet, four inches

six pounds, eight ounces

seven hours, twenty minutes

Use a comma to avoid misreading.

This final comma rule does not give permission to place commas anywhere you please. You should not add commas to sentences because the commas look good, sound good, or seem to reflect a pause. However, if a sentence simply does not make sense without a comma or if the comma clarifies the meaning, you may add the comma. Be careful, however. The comma must clearly prevent sentence confusion. Also, remember that adding a comma will never fix a poorly constructed sentence.

Unclear:	To Jane Robinson seemed handsome and suave.
Clear:	To Jane, Robinson seemed handsome and suave.
Unclear:	Those who can act quickly and decisively.
Clear:	Those who can, act quickly and decisively.
Unclear:	When angry camels spit.
Clear:	When angry, camels spit.

PRACTICE SET 10–8

Directions: In the following sentences, add commas where needed. Write "correct" next to sentences that need no commas.

Example: She used to live in Macon, Georgia.

1. The Summer Olympic Games were held in Sydney Australia.

2. According to the *Tribune* Jack O'Reilly D.D.S. is closing his dental office in Manchester Vermont.

3. On May 31 1995 they moved to 906 Christopher Street Dallas Texas 78706.

4. The premature baby weighed only three pounds six ounces at birth.

5. At four thirty soldiers left on patrol.

6. Last year 6532978 suitcases were checked by customs agents in Miami.

7. In spring showers occur frequently.

8. If lost children should find a trustworthy adult to ask for assistance.

9. The freak blizzard occurred in May 1999.

10. The flight from Los Angeles to Singapore lasted seven hours fifteen minutes.

TEST YOURSELF

Directions: In the following sentences, add commas where needed. Write "correct" next to sentences that need no commas.

1. Carole ordered sheets towels and blankets from the discount catalog.

2. People who use cell phones while driving run an increased risk of being involved in automobile accidents.

3. Even though the cook followed the recipe exactly the cake was dry and tasteless.

4. Eric received an MP3 player not a laptop computer from his grandparents for his birthday.

5. The toddler is very tired but she refuses to take a nap.

6. To win the election each candidate spent millions of dollars on television advertising.

7. The protesters marched without a permit and were therefore arrested by the police.

8. Chris is walking with a cane because he has recently had knee surgery.

9. *Law and Order* my father's favorite television show presents fictional stories based on real-life crimes.

10. On October 4 2005 Gina Calhoun M.D. opened a plastic surgery clinic in Athens Georgia.

COMPOSITION WARM-UP

Directions: In the following sentences, add commas where needed and be prepared to tell the rule that applies to each. Write "correct" next to sentences that need no commas.

Example: During the final act, everybody dies.

1. A person who can't balance a checkbook shouldn't try to run a business.

2. Her nephew is a rude obnoxious child.

3. People who have to leave the show at intermission.

4. Bill Gates for example gives millions to charity each year.

5. I didn't read the book nor did I see the movie.

6. I bought three new hairclips.

7. All Fido does is eat sleep and make a mess.

8. The candidate took office on January 10 2004 in Washington D.C.

9. Although he is my twin brother we do not look at all alike.

10. "I am leaving now" the nurse said quietly to the patient.

11. The driver his cell phone ringing loudly was easily distracted.

12. At the grand opening of the WalMart he read a poem about success.

13. Students who do not study usually do poorly in college.

14. I need your raincoat not your umbrella.

15. My father who owns a dry cleaning store was able to get the spot out of my dress.

16. New York my favorite city is very crowded in the spring.

17. He needed a haircut but didn't get one.

18. Meredith you are going to Los Angeles on business aren't you?

19. She analyzed the poem "Mending Wall" for her English assignment.

20. You know of course that she is not coming to the party.

21. In fact their bank account was seriously overdrawn.

22. Marcella said that the Writing Center needed additional assistants.

23. His term lasted from April 2004 to January 2005.

24. The basketball center for our college team is 7 feet 3 inches tall.

25. In the middle of a huge project at work the manager resigned.

COMPOSITION PRACTICE

Directions: Write a sentence requiring commas for each of the rules listed in the chapter, being sure to punctuate each correctly.

1. Use a comma before a coordinating conjunction that separates independent clauses.

2. Use commas to separate items in a series.

3. Use a comma after an introductory element.

4. Use commas appropriately for restrictive and nonrestrictive clauses and phrases.

5. Use commas to set off interrupting expressions.

6. Use commas to set off absolute constructions.

7. Use commas to set off direct quotations.

8. Use commas when appropriate for dates and addresses, names and titles, informal salutations, large numbers, and statistics.

9. Use a comma to avoid misreading.

WORD WATCHERS

Some words are considered substandard and should never be used in writing.

hisself/theirself	Substandard for *himself* and *themselves.*
irregardless	Substandard for *regardless.*
should of/would of/could of	The *of* in these phrases should be *have:* I should have saved my money (not I should of saved my money).
use to/suppose to	Substandard for *used to* and *supposed to.* Don't drop the *d:* He used to be my friend. He is supposed to be in class.
anywheres/nowheres	Substandard for *anywhere* and *nowhere.*

WORD WATCHERS PRACTICE SET

Directions: Choose the correct word in parentheses.

1. We will hold the picnic (regardless / irregardless) of the weather.

2. I would (of, have) become a famous singer if I could (of / have) sung on key.

3. They gave them the answers (theirselves / themselves).

4. She was (suppose / supposed) to meet me in the mall by lunchtime.

5. Scientists have not found life (anywhere / anywheres) on Jupiter.

(continued)

WORD WATCHERS
(cont.)

6. She should (of / have) listened to the directions more closely.

7. (Nowhere / Nowheres) in this building can I find an elevator.

8. Felix told me about the car crash (hisself / himself).

9. Carolyn and Glenna (use / used) to work for the FBI.

10. They gave (theirselves / themselves) a reason to believe the child's story.

Chapter 11

Other Punctuation and Capitalization

Semicolons

Use semicolons (;) to separate independent clauses and items in a series when the items themselves contain commas.

Use semicolons to separate independent clauses.

Semicolons come between two sentences that are relatively short and closely related in meaning. Basically, the semicolon takes the place of the comma and the coordinating conjunction. The second independent clause begins with a lowercase letter rather than a capital.

independent clause	coordinating conjunction	independent clause
This fern is drooping,	*so*	it must need water and fertilizer.

OR

independent clause	independent clause
This fern is drooping;	it must need water and fertilizer.

Transitional expressions often follow semicolons. Such expressions emphasize the type of relationship between the two independent clauses. Note that a comma always follows the transitional expression after the semicolon.

The following sentences show three different ways of punctuating independent clauses:

Comma + conjunction: The water is quite calm now, but a storm may be approaching later.

Semicolon: The water is quite calm now; a storm may be approaching later.

Semicolon + transitional expression + comma: The water is quite calm now; however, a storm may be approaching later.

Be careful, though. Not every transitional expression requires a semicolon. If the transitional expression appears in the middle of one independent clause, set it off with commas:

Incorrect: The building; however, was condemned.

Correct: The building, however, was condemned.

Study the following list of transitional expressions so that you can use them effectively for sentence variety.

Transitional expressions to indicate addition: *again, also, besides, equally important, finally, first, further, furthermore, in addition, last, likewise, moreover, next, second, third*

Transitional expressions to indicate cause and effect: *accordingly, as a result, consequently, hence, in short, otherwise, then, therefore, thus*

Transitional expressions to indicate contrast: *although true, for all that, however, in contrast, nevertheless, notwithstanding, on the contrary, on the other hand, still*

Transitional expressions to indicate similarity: *likewise, similarly*

Transitional expressions to indicate special features or examples: *for example, for instance, incidentally, indeed, in fact, in other words, in particular, specifically, that is, to be exact, to illustrate*

Transitional expressions to indicate summation: *in brief, in conclusion, in short, on the whole, to conclude, to summarize, to sum up, therefore, thus*

PRACTICE SET 11–1

Directions: Add commas or semicolons where needed in the following sentences.

Example: My son is a great baseball player; thus, he hopes to get an athletic scholarship.

1. I forgot to buy onions and tomato sauce consequently I was unable to make the casserole for the dinner party.

2. Living out of a suitcase however can become very tiring.

3. Justin is an outstanding writer in fact he won second place in the school's essay contest.

4. Mr. Jennings reminded Nick to pay the cable bill nevertheless he forgot to mail it before the due date.

5. Your first assignment for English therefore will be to study the comma rules in Chapter 10.

Don't confuse subordinating conjunctions with transitional expressions. Beginning sentences with words like *whereas*, *although*, and *because* and phrases like *such as* and *so* can create sentence fragments.

> **Incorrect:** She invited me to spend the night. Although, she had to work early the next morning.

> **Correct:** She invited me to spend the night although she had to work early the next morning.

Use semicolons to separate items in a series when the items themselves contain commas.

When the items in a series contain commas, use a semicolon to separate the items.

> This summer, we are planning to visit Barcelona, Spain; Lisbon, Portugal; and Paris, France.

Here, the use of the semicolon makes the meaning of the sentence clear.

PRACTICE SET 11–2

Directions: Add semicolons and/or commas where needed in the following sentences.

Example: Danny needs some new sneakers; however, he can't afford them right now.

1. School begins early this year classes start on August 15.

2. The following professionals spoke at the conference: Elise Garcia an architect Dave Brewster a space planner and Kathy Coleman an engineer.

3. I don't want to call you in fact I don't ever want to speak to you again.

4. Baby boomers are those people born between 1946 and 1964 seventy-eight million Americans fall into this category.

5. The Democrats control the Senate the Republicans control the House of Representatives.

6. She approached the podium and carefully arranged her notes then she began to speak.

7. The identical twins grew up in separate families nevertheless their habits and attitudes were very similar.

8. Trung held the delicate blossom in her hand she could smell its sweet fragrance.

9. The violent teenager will be tried as an adult thus he can be sentenced to life in prison.

10. Her credit card bill therefore is far too high for her to pay by herself.

Colons

Use colons in four special situations.

Use colons to separate independent clauses from other words, phrases, or clauses that rename or define the independent clauses.

The colon must be preceded by an independent clause, but it does not have to be followed by one.

Colon followed by an independent clause: The young man had one major goal: he wanted to go to college.

Colon followed by a phrase: The young man had one major goal: to go to college.

Colon followed by a single word: The young man had one major goal: college.

All of these sample sentences are correct because an independent clause comes before the colon and what comes after the colon defines or clarifies this clause.

Use colons to introduce lists or long series.

We need several items at the grocery store: eggs, milk, bread, and laundry detergent.

Often, expressions like *the following* or *as follows* introduce this list.

Stock dividends will be issued on the following dates: February 15, May 15, August 15, and November 15.

Be careful about the phrases *such as* and *like*. These are never followed by a colon.

Incorrect: I subscribe to several magazines, such as: *Newsweek, House Beautiful*, and *Skiing.*

Correct: I subscribe to several magazines, such as *Newsweek, House Beautiful*, and *Skiing.*

Use colons to introduce long or formal quotations.

In his inaugural address in January 1961, President John Fitzgerald Kennedy issued the following challenge to the American people: "Ask not what your country can do for you. Ask what you can do for your country."

Use colons to separate titles and subtitles, chapters and verses of biblical citations, hours and minutes. Also use a colon after the greeting of a formal letter.

A User's Guide to the Millennium: Essays and Reviews

Matthew 5:17

6:00 P.M.

Dear Professor Forbes:

 **Quick Tip**

Remember that a colon never separates a verb from its direct object or subject complement or a preposition from its object.

verb ┌──────── direct object ────────┐

Incorrect: We ordered: a new couch, dining room chairs, and a buffet.

Correct: We ordered a new couch, dining room chairs, and a buffet.

Correct: We ordered some new furniture: a couch, dining room chairs, and a buffet.

preposition objects

Incorrect: Richard has lived   in: Florida, Missouri, Pennsylvania, and Texas.

Correct: Richard has lived in Florida, Missouri, Pennsylvania, and Texas.

Correct: Richard has lived in the following states: Florida, Missouri, Pennsylvania, and Texas.

PRACTICE SET 11–3

Directions: Insert colons where needed in the following sentences. If a sentence is correct, write "correct" in the margin.

Example: We volunteered for three different jobs: painting, cleaning, and driving.

1. We accurately predicted the result Miss Florida won the pageant.

2. Rabbi Berger's favorite quotation comes from Isaiah 2 4. It reads as follows "They will beat their swords into plowshares and their spears into pruning hooks. Neither will they learn war anymore."

3. We can meet in the cafeteria at 7 15 tomorrow evening.

4. A wise hiker carries water, food, bandages, and insect repellent.

5. In addition to the textbook, you must purchase the following supplies for this course pencils, a spiral composition book, and a package of standard notebook paper.

6. Dear Dr. Shames

7. You can see some successful plays, such as *Cats* and *Les Misérables*, in performing arts centers throughout the United States.

8. I received a notice from the library that *Hollywood and Broadway A Study in Contrast* is a week overdue.

9. There are two words he always misspells *definitely* and *judgment.*

10. During the famous March on Washington on August 28, 1963, Dr. Martin Luther King, Jr., spoke some of his most memorable words "I have a dream that my four little children will one day live in a nation where they will not be judged by the color of their skin but by the content of their character."

End Punctuation

Use end punctuation marks, including periods, question marks, and exclamation points, to end a sentence.

Use periods (.) at the end of statements, commands, or requests.

> The baby is sleeping in the cradle near the fireplace.
>
> Answer his question.
>
> Please shut the door.

Use periods within and after certain abbreviations.

> *Mr.*, *Mrs.*, and *Ms.* are followed by a period. *Miss* is not. Abbreviations such as *Dr.*, *Sgt.*, *Ph.D.*, *St.*, *Ave.*, *B.C.E.*, *A.M.*, and *P.M.* have required periods. However, in modern usage, many writers omit the periods in *PhD*, *BCE*, *AM*, and *PM*.
>
> The abbreviations for the names of many organizations and government agencies no longer require periods.

AAA	DEA	FDA	NAACP	OPEC
ACLU	EPA	HUD	NATO	PTA
ASPCA	FBI	IRS	NOW	UNICEF

> Standard postal service abbreviations for state names do not contain periods.

> FL, GA, NC, NY, CA, AZ, TX, TN, CO

> If you are unclear about a particular abbreviation, consult a current dictionary. Another mark of punctuation, such as a comma or a question mark, may follow a period after an abbreviation, but a sentence can end with only one period.

> Since the assassination of Dr. Martin Luther King, Jr., many streets in the United States bear his name.
>
> Can you meet me as early as 6 A.M.?
>
> Nebuchadnezzar, the King of Babylonia, conquered Jerusalem in 586 B.C.E.

Use question marks (?) at the end of interrogative sentences, whether they are direct questions or echo questions.

> **Direct question:**　Can you baby-sit on Saturday evening?
>
> **Echo question:**　You can baby-sit on Saturday evening, can't you?

Use periods, not question marks, after indirect questions.

> **Indirect question:**　Jamie wondered whether she would be able to find an apartment for the summer.

Use exclamation points at the end of exclamatory statements, word groups, or strong interjections to express intense feeling or emotion.

Exclamatory statement:	I most certainly will not marry you!
Word group:	How wonderful!
Strong interjection:	Wow!

The expression *What a(n)* at the beginning of a sentence or word group usually indicates an exclamation.

What a terrific party that was!

What an exciting trip to take!

Composition Clue

Avoid overusing exclamation points in formal writing. They lose their effectiveness very quickly. Never use more than one exclamation point to end a sentence.

PRACTICE SET 11–4

Directions: Punctuate the following sentences using periods, question marks, and exclamation points.

Example: Are Svetlana and Rudy going ice-skating at the new rink downtown?

1. Has Professor Berry completed his dissertation for his Ph D

2. What a glorious sunset tonight

3. The sick old man wonders if he will ever leave the hospital

4. Most bank accounts in the U S are insured by the FDIC, aren't they

5. I am truly shocked by your crude language in class

Quotation Marks

Use quotation marks to set off a direct quotation.

A **direct quotation** repeats someone's exact speech.

Using other punctuation with quotation marks varies according to the placement and type of the quotation. Use the following examples as a guide.

Quotation follows introductory material: My friend Sally said, "Dave and I would like you to come for dinner on Sunday."

Quotation precedes explanatory material: "Dave and I would like you to come for dinner on Sunday," my friend Sally said.

Quotation includes question mark or exclamation point: "May I borrow two cups of flour?" my neighbor asked.

"I can't wait until graduation!" the excited student told her parents.

Quotation and sentence are both questions or exclamations: Did Shannon ask her father, "Can we go fishing this weekend?"

He shouted from the balcony, "I love you!"

Single sentence quotation divided by explanatory words: "I bought a microwave," Russell said, "because I never have time to cook."

If the quotation itself is more than one sentence, separate the sentences with end punctuation to avoid creating a run-on sentence.

Incorrect: "I'm going to bed early tonight," Nell said, "I was up late all weekend."

Correct: "I'm going to bed early tonight," Nell said. "I was up late all weekend."

Use single quotation marks to enclose a quotation within a quotation.

The apostrophe functions as a single quotation mark.

My daughter reminded me, "Remember Dad's favorite saying, 'You always get what you pay for.'"

Always place periods and commas inside closing quotation marks.

Ricky has easily memorized Carl Sandburg's short poem "Fog."

"I can't wait here any longer," the frustrated client said to the receptionist.

Always place colons and semicolons outside quotation marks.

His favorite hymn is "Amazing Grace"; he especially loves hearing it played on bagpipes.

There are only two characters in Poe's famous story "The Tell-tale Heart": the murderer and the victim.

Place question marks and exclamation points inside or outside, depending on the sentence.

Quotation is a question: MacKenzie asked, "How are you?"

Sentence is a question but quotation is not: Did Merrill say, "You are fired"?

Sentence and quotation are both questions: Why did she ask, "How old are you?"

Be careful to distinguish direct quotations from indirect ones. An **indirect quotation** simply paraphrases someone's words and does not require quotation marks.

Direct quotation: My doctor said, "Take two aspirin and call me in the morning."

Indirect quotation: My doctor told me to take two aspirin and call him in the morning.

Use quotation marks around the titles of short works, such as poems, songs, articles, short stories, speeches, episodes of particular television shows, and chapters in a book.

The English professor's favorite short story is "The Lesson" by Toni Cade Bambara.

"The Wedding" was one of the most popular episodes on the television series *Friends*.

Do not use quotation marks around the title of your own paper on the original manuscript.

Use quotation marks to set off words used in a special sense.

Is this band playing what my grandparents call "swing" music?

Use an ellipsis to show that some material has been omitted from a direct quotation.

An ellipsis is three spaced periods appearing together. This punctuation is effective in condensing a long quotation that contains more information or words than the writer wants to quote. If the omission appears at the end of the quotation, use four periods—three for the ellipsis and one for the end of the sentence. After the ellipsis, the rest of the quotation must be logical and grammatically correct.

The following quotations are excerpts from Abraham Lincoln's "Gettysburg Address." The first one is a complete quotation. The second one contains several ellipses marking the omission of words.

Complete quotation: "We are met on a great battlefield of that war. We have come to dedicate a portion of that field, as a final resting place for those who here gave their lives that that nation might live."

Quotation containing omissions: "We are met on a great battlefield . . . to dedicate a portion of that field, as a final resting place for those who here gave their lives. . . ."

Use brackets to insert words of your own into quotations for explanation, clarity, or grammatical correctness.

"We are met on a great battlefield [Gettysburg] of that war."

PRACTICE SET 11–5

Directions: Punctuate the following sentences, using whatever kind of punctuation is needed.

Example: "Let's go to the zoo tomorrow afternoon," LeAnne suggested.

1. Would you like pancakes for breakfast Mr. Lunsford asked his children

2. I need some help with my research paper the student said to the librarian I can't find anything on my topic

3. Flannery O'Connor once wrote The peculiar problem of the short-story writer is how to make the action he describes reveal as much of the mystery of existence as possible

4. Have you ever read Robert Frost's poem Fire and Ice

5. My car has a dead battery the frustrated driver reported to the AAA operator and I need a jump-start immediately

6. Andre Dubus's short story Killings describes a grieving father's act of revenge

7. Help me the frightened man screamed from the balcony of the burning building

8. The first episode of *CSI* was called Cool Change

9. Did I hear Brenda ask What time is my last appointment

10. In the nursery school program, the children sang Itsy Bitsy Spider and The Wheels on the Bus

Italics

Use italics to note certain titles.

With a computer or word processor, creating italics is easy. If you are using a typewriter or writing by hand, underlining substitutes for italicizing.

Italicize the titles of long works: books, plays, long poems, essays, pamphlets, newspapers, magazines, operas, movies, television series, radio programs, albums, paintings, and sculptures.

Books: *Wuthering Heights, Huckleberry Finn*

Plays: *The Piano Lesson, Six Degrees of Separation*

Long poems: *Beowulf, Song of Roland*

Essays: *Self-Reliance, A Defense of Poetry*

Pamphlets: *Common Sense, Ten Early Warning Signs of Cancer*

Newspapers: *Atlanta Journal, Detroit Free Press*

Magazines and journals: *Better Homes and Gardens, Journal of Modern Psychiatry*

Operas: *Carmen, Aïda*

Movies: *The Terminator, Pretty Woman*

Television series: *Law and Order, Will and Grace*

Radio programs: *All Things Considered, Prairie Home Companion*

Musical recordings—albums or CDs: *The Eagles' Greatest Hits, The Nylon Curtain*

Paintings: *Starry Night, Guernica*

Sculptures: *The Thinker, Venus de Milo*

Do not italicize the names of sacred books or their sections.

the Bible, Luke, Psalms

Do not italicize the names of legal documents.

Constitution, Declaration of Independence, Bill of Rights

Italicize the names of particular ships, planes, trains, and spacecraft.

Titanic, Spirit of St. Louis, City of New Orleans, Challenger

Italicize foreign words that have not become a standard part of contemporary English.

The abbreviation *R.S.V.P.* stands for the French expression *Répondez, s'il vous plaît,* which means "Answer, please."

Italicize words, phrases, letters, and numbers used as words.

In a dictionary with small print, distinguishing a dotted *i* from a lowercase *l* is often difficult.

Students often confuse the spelling of *there, their,* and *they're.*

In today's society is a meaningless, overused expression.

Do not italicize or underline the title of your own paper on the original manuscript.

Hyphens

Use hyphens (-) to separate.

In most instances, whether to use a hyphen is a spelling consideration rather than a grammatical one. If you have questions about hyphen use, consult a current dictionary. However, there are some rules that you should apply consistently.

Use hyphens in fractions.

Management fired one-half of the staff.

Use hyphens for compound numbers.

Hyphenate compound numbers, such as *thirty-seven* or *fifty-three*. Do not hyphenate numbers like *one hundred, five thousand,* or *ten million.*

three hundred fifty-four dollars

Use hyphens between two words used together to form a compound adjective only when the compound adjective comes before the noun it modifies.

Rod Stewart, Elton John, and Mick Jagger are *world-famous* rock singers.

The rock singers Rod Stewart, Elton John, and Mick Jagger are *world famous*.

Do not use hyphens between adverbs ending in *ly* and adjectives.

I posted a *clearly written* notice on the employee bulletin board.

Use hyphens with prefixes such as *ex, self,* and *all* and the suffix *elect*.

My *ex-wife* is *president-elect* of the garden club.

Use hyphens with prefixes before proper nouns or adjectives.

He testified before the House *Un-American* Activities Committee in *mid-July*.

Quick Tip

Many writers use hyphens to divide words of two or more syllables at the end of a line if the completed word extends beyond the margin. This practice can cause confusion and spelling errors. If you must divide a word, consult a dictionary so that you can divide the word correctly. Fortunately, using computers and word processors eliminates this problem.

Dashes

Use dashes (—) to link information.

A dash is two hyphens typed together with no space between, before, or after. In formal writing, use dashes sparingly. However, using a dash is appropriate for appositives or other parenthetical expressions that contain internal commas or that should be set off for strong emphasis.

Three members of my family—Aunt Loretta, Uncle Marshall, and Cousin Francine—were born in Chicago.

Rich desserts, snack foods, and alcohol—these are a dieter's downfall.

Parentheses

Use parentheses to enclose information.

In informal writing, writers use parentheses to enclose information that is extra, humorous, or out of logical order. Avoid parentheses in formal writing. However, parentheses are required in the following situations:

Use parentheses to enclose birth and/or death years following a person's name.

Rose Kennedy (1890–1995), the matriarch of the Kennedy family, outlived four of her nine children.

Use parentheses to enclose publication dates, page numbers, or other documentation information.

Dr. Jekyll and Mr. Hyde (1886), a short novel by Robert Louis Stevenson, is also a film and a musical play.

Use parentheses around numbers that list a series.

Mrs. Rodriguez wants to sell her home because (1) it is too large for one person, (2) it is too expensive to maintain, and (3) the property taxes have doubled in the last five years.

Place commas, periods, semicolons, and colons outside the parentheses unless the parenthetical material is a complete sentence that requires its own end punctuation.

Hamlet's soliloquy begins, "To be, or not to be; that is the question" (*Hamlet,* 1.3.56).

I had to borrow Natasha's jacket when it turned cold. (I had left mine at the restaurant.)

PRACTICE SET 11–6

Directions: Punctuate the following sentences using hyphens, dashes, parentheses, and underlining (italics).

> Example: Henry David Thoreau (1817–1862) wrote the essay <u>Civil Disobedience</u> (1849) to explain his refusal to pay a government poll tax.

1. Roses, azaleas, and begonias all of these plants are on sale at Plant World this weekend.

2. Charles Lindbergh 1902 1974 is remembered for 1 his solo flight across the Atlantic Ocean, 2 his highly conservative politics, and 3 the kidnapping and murder of his infant son.

3. South Pacific, Miss Saigon, and M. Butterfly these contemporary plays have certain similarities to the Puccini opera Madama Butterfly.

4. My subscriptions to Newsweek, Architectural Digest, and Southern Living expire in December.

5. Telemarker is a term used to describe a skier who skis downhill using cross country style equipment.

6. Professor Adams will mark the exams by mid May.

7. We board our three pets the cat, the dog, and the hamster when we leave on vacation.

8. The snowboarder's brightly colored hair made him a well known figure in the lodge at Park City.

9. On Thanksgiving Day, the volunteers at the soup kitchen served seventy five breakfasts, ninety two lunches, and two hundred dinners.

10. In The Feminine Mystique 1963, writer Betty Friedan encouraged women to be themselves and achieve their own goals without giving up either marriage or a family.

Apostrophes

Use apostrophes appropriately.

An apostrophe looks like a single quotation mark. Use apostrophes in the following situations:

Use apostrophes to show possession or ownership.

> Jennifer found *Jill's wallet* under the front seat of the car. (The wallet belongs to Jill.)
>
> We stacked the *children's games* in the closet. (The games belong to the children.)

While it is easy to see possession when something *belongs* to someone, possession also means that something is *of* something else.

Tomorrow's lecture will be about apostrophes. (the lecture *of* tomorrow)

He deserves a *day's pay* for a *day's work*. (the pay *of* a day for the work *of* a day)

Water from the flowers spilled onto the antique *book's cover*. (the cover *of* the book)

Apostrophes also show ownership with indefinite pronouns.

someone's raincoat   everybody's business   another's theory

Use apostrophes to form the plurals of letters, numbers, symbols, and words used as words.

A dyslexic individual often confuses *b*'s and *d*'s.

My Social Security number has five *6*'s in it.

You should not use *&*'s in formal writing.

Be careful about using too many *and*'s in a sentence.

Notice that the *s* is not italicized in these plural forms.

Quick Tip

Some sources suggest using a lowercase *s* without an apostrophe for numbers and abbreviations.

TVs appeared in many homes in the 1950s.

If omitting the apostrophe causes confusion, leave it in.

Confusing: I made three As last term.

Clear: I made three A's last term.

Use apostrophes to take the place of missing letters in contractions or dates.

cannot = can't   does not = doesn't

he is = he's   would not = wouldn't

they are = they're   1993 = '93

One of the difficulties with apostrophes is deciding whether to place them before the *s* or after the *s*. Note the following rules:

- **For plural possessives, make the noun plural before adding the apostrophe.**

Possessive Noun	Rule	Example
singular, does not end in *s*	add apostrophe + *s*	one girl's project the baby's toys
singular, ends in *s*	add apostrophe + *s* or just apostrophe*	Ross's job Yeats's poetry or Yeats' poetry
plural, ends in *s*	add apostrophe	four girls' projects families' commitments
plural, doesn't end in *s*	apostrophe + *s*	children's music women's lounge

*Most authorities recommend going by pronunciation: if you say the extra syllable in the possessive, then you add *s*.

- **With compounds, showing possession and number varies.**

Compound	Rule	Example
single words showing joint possession	add apostrophe + *s* or just apostrophe to final noun	Elaine and Benny's adventure Kim and James' sailboat
single words showing separate possession	add apostrophe + *s* or just an apostrophe to each noun	Ray's and Scott's video games James' and Charles' homes
compound words showing possession	add apostrophe + *s* to the final word	my brother-in-law's car the attorney general's argument
plural compound words	add *s* to the first word	two brothers-in-law two attorneys general
plural compound words showing possession	add *s* to the first word and apostrophe + *s* to the last word	two brothers-in-law's cars two attorneys general's arguments

Learn when not to use apostrophes.

Do not use an apostrophe to form the possessives of personal pronouns.

Incorrect: The book is her's.

Correct: The book is hers.

Incorrect: That picnic spot is our's.

Correct: That picnic spot is ours.

Do not use an apostrophe in the word *its* if you mean *belonging to it. It's* always means *it is.*

Incorrect: The zebra lost it's stripes.

Correct: The zebra lost its stripes.

Incorrect: Its going to rain.

Correct: It's going to rain.

Do not add apostrophes to verbs ending in *s.*

Incorrect: Megan cook's us breakfast.

Correct: Megan cooks us breakfast.

Do not use apostrophes to make nouns plural.

Incorrect: I bought several bathing suit's.

Correct: I bought several bathing suits.

Do not make titles possessive.

Incorrect: "Reunion's" setting is New York City.

Correct: The setting of "Reunion" is New York City.

PRACTICE SET 11–7

Directions: Add apostrophes where needed in the following sentences.

Example: For the parade, the trainer braided the horse's mane and tail with colorful ribbons.

1. The anniversary party will be at Ellie and Elliotts house on Saturday night.

2. How many *i* s are there in the word *Mississippi?*

3. We are painting the ladies dressing room yellow and the childrens playroom dark green.

4. Its too late to submit your painting for its admission to the art show.

5. The employees contributed two weeks salary to the annual United Way campaign.

6. The hospital staff has upgraded her sister-in-laws condition from *critical* to *fair*.

7. The ducks tails were bobbing in the rough water.

8. Nicole graduated from high school in 96.

9. Jeans and Susans puppies come from the same litter.

10. The party organizer put a small favor by everyones plate at the banquet table.

Capitalization

Capitalize appropriately.

Capitalization is making the first letter of a word uppercase.

Capitalize the first word of any sentence, question, or exclamation.

We should replace the carpet in the dining room.

Is it still raining?

What a brilliant idea!

Capitalize the first word of a direct quotation if the quotation is a complete sentence.

The dean replied, "Classes begin on January 8."

Capitalize all proper nouns—the names of specific persons, places, or things.

Jane Doe	Lowry Park	Plaza Hotel
Plant High School	Lake Lure	Majestic Theater
Rome, Georgia	Asia	Brooklyn Bridge
Bay Way Drive	Indian Ocean	Medal of Honor

Capitalize titles that appear before names and the titles of heads of state.

Chancellor Gwendolyn Stephenson	Doctor Seth Mabry
Judge Christine Nguyen	Chairman Mao Zedong
Uncle Dave	President George W. Bush

Capitalize a title if it substitutes for a name.

We will meet Mother at 6:30 for dinner, and my grandfather will probably join us.

Capitalize the personal pronoun *I*.

The mechanic did not seem to understand what I was telling him.

Capitalize the names of all sacred books and of races, nationalities, languages, religions and their followers.

New Testament	African-American	British	Farsi
Koran	Buddhism	Caucasian	Korean
French	Muslims	Hispanic	Judaism
Hindi	Vietnamese	Islam	Latin

Capitalize the names of deities.

People worship God in various ways.

Capitalize the titles of specific courses of study.

Do not capitalize a general school subject (algebra, biology, economics, history) unless it is a language or is followed by a course number.

Because I enjoy English and math courses, I am taking Linguistics 1670 and Calculus 406.

Capitalize the names of historical documents and periods of historical significance.

Renaissance	Industrial Revolution	Magna Carta
Ice Age	Civil War	Treaty of Versailles
Paleozoic Era	World War II	Bill of Rights

Capitalize the first word and all important words in a title.

Do not capitalize the articles (*a, an, the*) or short prepositions and conjunctions unless they appear first in the title.

A Shot in the Dark, The Grapes of Wrath, In the Heat of the Night, Of Mice and Men, "A Good Man Is Hard to Find"

Capitalize the names of specific businesses, organizations, and teams.

Target	Girl Scouts of America
The Critter Shop	Chicago Cubs
Red Cross	University of Texas Longhorns
National Organization for Women	Atlanta Falcons

Capitalize brand names but not the item.

Kleenex tissue, Colgate toothpaste, Quaker oatmeal, Nabisco graham crackers

Capitalize the days of the week, the months of the year, and the names of holidays and special events.

Monday	Memorial Day	Mother's Day
Saturday	Fourth of July	Super Bowl
June	Easter	Winter Olympics

Do not capitalize the names of the seasons unless they are part of the name of a particular event.

We cut back our rosebushes in winter.

In March or April, students at the University of Pennsylvania celebrate Spring Fling.

Capitalize the names of the planets.

Mercury, Venus, Earth, Mars, Jupiter, Saturn, Uranus, Neptune, and Pluto revolve around the sun in the Milky Way Galaxy.

If Earth is listed specifically as a planet, as in the sentence above, capitalize it. If it is otherwise mentioned, do not capitalize it.

Many parts of the earth have become overpopulated and polluted.

Capitalize the names of particular areas of the United States.

People born in the South usually have strong feelings of regional loyalty.

Do not capitalize directions.

To reach the mall, drive south on Westshore Boulevard.

PRACTICE SET 11–8

Directions: Add capital letters where needed in the following sentences.

Example: when grocery shopping at albertson's, peter usually buys tropicana

orange juice and breakstone sour cream.

1. many christians who live in palestine now speak hebrew, arabic, and english.

2. in april, i spoke with mayor pam iorio at the annual fundraiser for metropolitan ministries of hillsborough county.

3. in *a tale of two cities,* charles dickens describes the year 1775, prior to the french revolution, as follows: "it was the best of times, it was the worst of times."

4. recently, droughts and floods in the west have had disastrous consequences.

5. to complete his science and humanities requirements, jonathan has registered for applied physics 102 and art history 203.

6. we gave grandma and grandpa a family photograph for hanukkah.

7. on saturday, albert is going to auto kingdom to have his tires checked.

8. during registration, my advisor urged me to check with professor martinez about my spanish grade.

9. the scholarship is designated for hispanic females who want to major in business at the university of south florida.

10. in the summer of 1990, reverend and mrs. miller, who lived in the northeast, drove west toward the rocky mountains of colorado.

Abbreviations, Symbols, and Numbers

Abbreviate appropriately.

Abbreviations are shortened forms of words.

Common abbreviations for titles used with names are acceptable in formal writing.

Mr., Mrs., Dr., Rev., Gen., Sr., Jr., J.D., Esq., M.D., Ph.D., D.O.

Commonly understood abbreviations for organizations, departments of government, and technical terms are acceptable in formal writing.

YMCA	NYSE	NCAA	NFL
NBA	UN	FDA	RAM
NBC	CIA	FCC	VCR
RCA	NLRB	VA	CD
GOP	FAA	AIDS	TV

Composition Clue

☞

If you want to use a more obscure abbreviation in a paper, write out the full name the first time that you mention it, and put the abbreviation in parentheses after it. Then you can use the abbreviation alone for subsequent references.

Senator Graham's assistant will attend the next meeting of the Southwest Florida Water Management District (SWFWMD).

In formal writing, avoid most abbreviations of names, amounts, dates, and places.

Incorrect: During X-Mas vacation in NY, Jos. gained ten lbs. because he ate dinner late in the P.M. and had no time to exercise in the A.M.

Correct: During Christmas vacation in New York, Joseph gained ten pounds because he ate dinner late in the evening and had no time to exercise in the morning.

Although Latin abbreviations, such as *i.e.*, *e.g.*, and *etc.*, are acceptable in documentation and informal writing, avoid them in formal writing.

Incorrect: Gardeners must replant petunias, pansies, marigolds, *etc.* every spring.

Correct: Gardeners must replant annuals like petunias, pansies, and marigolds every spring.

Use only acceptable symbols in formal writing.

- **Use a dollar sign with dollar amounts that are too long to write out.**

  Incorrect: I paid five hundred thirty-six dollars and twenty cents for my computer.

  Correct: I paid $536.20 for my computer.

- **Do not use a dollar sign to write out simple dollar amounts.**

  Incorrect: I sold my old computer for $500.

  Correct: I sold my old computer for five hundred dollars.

- **Be consistent with percentages throughout a paper. Write out** *percent* **or use % every time.**

- **Do not use an ampersand (&) or a cent sign (¢) in formal writing.**

Follow standard rules when writing numbers.

Write out a number that begins a sentence.

> Three starlings have built a nest in the eaves of the porch.

If this situation is awkward because the number beginning the sentence is long, rephrase the sentence.

> **Incorrect:** 119 errors appeared in the accountant's tax records.
>
> **Correct:** The accountant's tax records contained 119 errors.

Remain consistent in form when using numbers in the same sentence, particularly when some numbers would normally be spelled out while others would not.

> Last week, Randy sold only 20 candy bars, but this week he has sold 127.

Use numbers in dates, times using A.M. and P.M., addresses, telephone listings, fractions, percentages, decimals, scores, statistics, money, divisions of books and plays, and identification numbers.

> The baby was born at 6:40 A.M. on July 20, 1970, and weighed 6 pounds, 9 ounces.
>
> The final game of the World Series was tied 4–4 at the beginning of the ninth inning.

PRACTICE SET 11–9

Directions: Correct the errors in abbreviations and numbers in the following sentences.

Example: ~~Chas.~~ _{Charles} Simone owns ~~6~~ _{six} different homes.

1. 40 students signed up for a class that should register only 25.

2. Leslie always mixes berries & cream with her breakfast cereal.

3. My son is a Dr., and he is interning at MA General Hosp. in Boston.

4. The study showed that fifty percent of the law school class were females and that 25% of the class were minority students.

5. I can't believe that Donald's car payment is six hundred and fifty dollars and thirty cents a month.

TEST YOURSELF

Directions: There is an error in punctuation or capitalization in each of the following sentences. Find and correct these mistakes.

1. The concert lasted for two hours, then the band played some songs that the audience requested.

2. Shakespeare's play "Romeo and Juliet" is often the basis for modern productions about ill-fated lovers.

3. Mushroom, pepperoni, and cheese; these are the boys' favorite kinds of pizza.

4. Professor Kim's Economics classes will be limited to business majors only.

5. The possum hid it's babies under the deck in our backyard.

6. We bought emergency supplies, such as: batteries, bottled water, candles, and canned food.

7. The librarian asked if Kristen wanted to check out the book she was reading?

8. "Will dinner be ready soon," Max asked his grandmother.

9. *Theme for English B,* a poem written by Langston Hughes, explores the relationship between student and teacher.

10. The mens' locker room is located at the end of the hall.

COMPOSITION WARM-UP

Directions: Add all punctuation marks and capitalization needed in the following paragraph. You may add any punctuation except commas.

Hillary Clinton is making her mark as an influential woman in the new millennium. In the August 01 issue of vanity fair magazine, Gail Sheehy, author of the best selling book passages, writes about Hillary Rodham Clinton. In an article entitled Hillary's solo act, Sheehy describes Clintons role as a US senator. Hillary clinton is an extremely hard working, ambitious, and intelligent woman. Graduate of yale law school, partner in a prestigious little rock, AR, law firm, and wife of a former governor, senator Clinton has long been close to power and powerful people. Of course, she is most widely known for her role as first lady of the US 1993–2001 and wife of one of the most controversial US presidents, William Jefferson Clinton. As first lady, Hillary Clinton played an active part in her husbands political career, directing much of his campaigning, promoting legislation, traveling, and speaking widely on issues important to her. Certainly, hillary clinton has forged a new path and altered most americans concept of the role of the presidents wife. Her place in the history books is assured. She is the best selling author of it takes a village, a former presidents wife, and the first first lady ever to leave the white house for the US senate.

COMPOSITION PRACTICE

Directions: Write a sentence requiring commas for each of the rules listed in the chapter, being sure to punctuate each correctly.

1. Write a sentence using a semicolon to separate two independent clauses.

2. Write a sentence using a colon to introduce a list.

3. Write a sentence using the phrase "such as" to introduce a list.

4. Write a sentence ending with a period and quotation marks.

5. Write a sentence containing a comma and quotation marks.

6. Write a sentence in which a quotation is part of a question.

7. Write a question ending with a quotation that is not part of the question.

8. Write a sentence containing an indirect quotation.

9. Write a sentence spelling out a fraction.

10. Write a sentence containing a compound adjective that comes before the word it modifies.

WORD WATCHERS

Pronouns can be confusing. Choose them carefully.

it's/its	*It's* is the contraction *it is:* It's true that my father is remarrying.
	Its is a possessive pronoun meaning *belonging to it:* The puppy wagged its tail.
there/their/they're	*There* has two uses. It is an adverb telling where: My book is over there.
	It is an expletive, part of the *there is/there are* construction: There is no excuse for that behavior.
	Their is a possessive pronoun meaning *belonging to them:* They paid for their own meals.
	They're is the contraction of *they are:* They're leaving for home tomorrow.
who/which/that	*Who* refers to people.
	Which and *that* refer to things and sometimes groups or classes of people. Don't use *which* or *that* to refer to a person: The student who (not *that*) plagiarized the paper was expelled.
who's/whose	*Who's* is the contraction of *who is:* Who's knocking at the door?
	Whose is a possessive pronoun meaning *belongs to whom:* Whose jacket is this?
which/witch	*Which* is a relative pronoun: My watch, which is broken, tells the correct time twice a day.
	A *witch* is a follower of Wicca or a woman with magical powers: In Arthur Miller's play *The Crucible,* Rebecca Nurse is accused of being a witch.
you're/your	*You're* is the contraction of *you are. Your* is a possessive pronoun: You're correct in your assumption.

(continued)

WORD WATCHERS PRACTICE SET

Directions: Choose the correct word in the parentheses.

1. (It's / Its) true that the two movie stars will be married in May.

2. Marlon's motorcycle, (witch / which) is still in the repair shop, may need a new motor.

3. I found a doctor (who's / whose) older than I am.

4. (There / Their / They're) is a lock on the door, so we can't get in.

5. If (your / you're) certain that the dog has been spayed, I will adopt him from the pound.

6. Babysitters (who / which / that) have more than three years of experience can command high salaries.

7. Lindsay and Calvin left for San Francisco in (there / their / they're) camper this morning.

8. The company filed for (it's / its) exemption before the deadline.

9. The partner (who's / whose) name is on the door commands the most respect.

10. (There / Their / They're) the ones who will suffer if the measurements are incorrect.

Chapter 12

Subject/Verb Agreement

Subject/verb agreement means that the subject and the verb match in number. Singular subjects match singular verb forms, and plural subjects match plural verb forms. Review the following list of singular and plural pronouns.

Personal pronoun subjects have three forms: first person, second person, and third person. They may be singular or plural.

	Singular	Plural
first person (the person speaking)	I	we
second person (the person spoken to)	you	you
third person (the person or object spoken about)	he, she, it	they

Verbs that appear with these pronouns must match them in number. Agreement is most often a problem with third person nouns or pronouns. The following rules will help you make subjects and verbs agree.

The -s ending often determines agreement.

Subject/verb agreement begins with an understanding of the -s ending. If you were asked, "How do you make a word plural?" you might be tempted to answer, "Add an s." While adding an s works for most nouns, it does not work for verbs. In fact, adding an s to a verb creates a singular form. Look at these two sentences:

Singular form: The dog barks.

Plural form: The dogs bark.

In the first sentence, the subject is singular and matches a singular verb form. Notice that only the verb ends in *s*. In the second sentence, the plural subject matches the plural verb form, and only the subject ends in *s*. Generally, only one of the words ends in *s*, either the subject or the verb. However, there are some important exceptions to this rule. Sometimes a singular noun ends in *s*:

> S   V
> The *glass falls* on the floor.

Other times, plural nouns don't end in *s*: *children, women, sheep.* Then, neither the subject nor the verb ends in *s*.

> S   V
> The *children play* in the park.

PRACTICE SET 12–1

Directions: Circle the correct verb in parentheses.

Example: These tires (has /(have)) no tread.

1. The soldiers (follows / follow) the captain's instructions.

2. Great opportunities (exists / exist) in education today.

3. I hope that the snow (lasts / last) until we can build a snowman.

4. Charles (agrees / agree) with your sister.

5. The milk (tastes / taste) sour.

6. Cheese slices (goes / go) great on a hamburger.

7. The rain-drenched children (comes / come) into the dry, warm room.

8. Small puzzle pieces (was / were) scattered around the room.

9. The money issues (has / have) affected our relationship.

10. Mrs. Jones (favors / favor) the health care plan.

Words that come between the subject and the verb do not change subject/verb agreement.

The verb must always agree with the subject, no matter where the subject comes in the sentence. Pay particular attention to prepositional phrases. The subject of the sentence is **never** part of a prepositional phrase. To avoid confusion, cross out all prepositional phrases before you identify the subject.

The *basket* ~~(of apples)~~ *falls* ~~(on the floor)~~.

~~(Over the river)~~ and ~~(through the woods)~~ ~~(to grandmother's house)~~ *we go.*

Certain prepositions consist of more than one word. These can be especially confusing because they make the sentence sound as if it has a plural subject. These prepositions include *along with*, *as well as*, *in addition to*, and *together with*. Cross them out just as you would single-word prepositions.

The *cat*, ~~(along with the kittens)~~, *sleeps* ~~(by the fireplace)~~~~(in the den)~~.

The *boat*, ~~(in addition to the automobiles)~~, *requires* insurance.

Other intervening words, phrases, or clauses do not change subject/verb agreement.

SC
My *mother*, **who loves to give instructions,** *is* usually right.

verbal phrase
The *train* **carrying the secret documents** *is* late.

appositive
Sophia Ramirez, **the treasurer and parliamentarian**, *enjoys* attending club activities.

PRACTICE SET 12–2

Directions: Circle the correct verb in parentheses.

Example: A house that has large closets ((sells)/ sell) quickly.

1. Apple pie, along with chocolate cookies and pumpkin cheesecake, (completes / complete) the huge Thanksgiving feast.

2. Michael Alan, who is a very loyal Buccaneers fan, (attends / attend) every home game.

3. A restaurant with no desserts (is / are) not usually successful.

4. Tiger Woods, who competes against the best golfers, frequently (wins / win).

5. Her goal to win five gold medals (has / have) become a reality.

6. My 1928 Chevy, in addition to your Model-T Ford, (shows / show) the beauty of well-made antique cars.

7. An essay containing numerous mechanical errors (receives / receive) a low grade.

8. A dog that destroys the furniture and newspapers (needs / need) training.

9. Her need to buy groceries (outweighs / outweigh) her desire to buy a new shirt.

10. The picture of daffodils (was / were) hanging in the hallway.

Compound subjects joined by *and* are usually plural.

Compound subjects are two or more simple subjects joined by *and.*

Francie and Murray ski in Colorado in the winter.

Honesty and integrity work together to build character.

PRACTICE SET 12–3

Directions: Circle the correct verb in parentheses.

Example: Sandy Beach and its surrounding suburbs often (floods /(flood)) during the rainy season.

1. The end of the fifth inning and the beginning of the sixth (was / were) exciting to watch.

2. The rosebush and the oak tree (requires / require) trimming.

3. His sneaky schemes and his ability to cover his tracks (makes / make) him a successful thief.

4. Her beautiful voice and good looks (assures / assure) that she will win the pageant.

5. To get a good job, be sure that your resumé and your clothing (is / are) up to date.

Note the following exceptions to the compound rules.

1. Some compounds joined by *and* appear plural but really refer to a single unit, like *ham and cheese* or *president and chief executive officer*. These compounds are singular.

   S   V
   My *best friend and traveling companion* **is** Elizabeth.

   S   V
   Macaroni and cheese **goes** well with hot dogs.

2. When *each* or *every* appears before a compound subject, the sentence takes a singular verb form.

   S   V
   Each test score and lab report **counts** toward the grade in the course.

   S   V
   Every man, woman, and child **participates** in the lifeboat drill.

Quick Tip

When *each* follows a compound subject, the subject takes a plural verb form.

          S   V

Robin and Jeffrey each ***want*** to go on a cruise.

3. Sometimes a compound subject is joined by *either/or, neither/nor, not only/but also* or by *or* or *nor*. In this case the verb agrees with the subject nearer to it.

                   nearer subject   verb
Either Katherine or   Don   ***plays*** tennis for the college team.

                   nearer subject verb
Buses, vans, or   limos   ***transport*** the hotel guests to the airport.

                nearer subject verb
Neither Tien nor her sisters ***attend*** school at night.

Quick Tip

                              S   V
Neither the kittens nor the *cat* ***sleeps*** on the bed.

The verb of this sentence, *sleeps*, agrees with *cat*, the subject nearer to it, but placing the singular subject second is awkward. When using singular and plural subjects together, try to place the plural subject closer to the verb.

                         S   V

Better: Neither the cat nor the kittens sleep on the bed.

PRACTICE SET 12–4

Directions: Circle the correct verb in parentheses.

Example: Either Brianna or her brothers (sells /(sell)) hot dogs at the ballpark.

1. Each representative and senator (has / have) agreed to participate in the program.

2. His only companion and friend (is / are) his golden retriever, Max.

3. Every dish, bowl, and glass (needs / need) to be washed carefully.

4. Neither the printer nor the computers (was / were) delivered on time.

5. Louisa and Alexandra each (is / are) leaving for New York this evening.

6. Lemonade, iced tea, or apple juice (tastes / taste) good on a hot summer day.

7. Not only the newspaper but also the radio bulletin (warns / warn) of the approaching hurricane.

8. Spaghetti and meatballs (appears / appear) on the menu in most Italian restaurants.

9. Each car seat, stroller, and high chair (was / were) carefully tested for safety.

10. Both Elvis Presley and John Lennon (is / are) mourned by millions of music fans.

Indefinite pronouns can be singular or plural.

Indefinite pronouns are those that do not refer to specific persons, places, or things. Because some are singular and some are plural, writers often make agreement errors using them. To help in this area, study the following chart closely.

Always Singular	Always Plural	Singular or Plural
one, each, another	both	some
either, neither	few	none
everyone, everybody, everything	several	any
someone, somebody, something	many	all
anyone, anybody, anything		more
no one, nobody, nothing		most

Some indefinite pronouns are always singular.

Pronouns that are always singular include words that end in *-one*, *-body*, and *-thing*: *anyone, anybody, anything, someone, somebody, something, no one, nobody, nothing.*

>   S   V
> *Anybody* **has** the option to retake the quiz.

The pronouns that are always singular also include *each, either, neither, another, one.*

>   S   V
> *Neither* **wants** to cook dinner this evening.

Quick Tip

Remember to ignore prepositional phrases that come between the subject and the verb:

Neither ~~(of the roommates)~~ wants to cook dinner this evening.

The subject of the sentence is *neither,* not *roommates. Neither* is always singular, so the verb must match.

Some indefinite pronouns are always plural.

Pronouns that are always plural include *both, few, several,* and *many.*

> *Many* **are** called, but *few* **are** chosen.

Sometimes an indefinite pronoun relies on its antecedent to determine whether the pronoun is singular or plural.

The antecedent is usually the object of the preposition in the phrase that follows the pronoun. These indefinite pronouns include *all, any, more, most, none,* and *some.*

> S   V
> *All* of the wine ***is*** chilled.

(In this sentence, *All* refers to the singular object of the preposition, *wine.*)

> S   V
> *All* of the hamburgers ***are*** hot.

(In this sentence, *All* refers to the plural object of the preposition, *hamburgers.*)

PRACTICE SET 12–5

Directions: Circle the correct verb in parentheses.

Example: Many of the animals (was / were) evacuated during the hurricane.

1. Some of the high-tech sound systems (confuses / confuse) the average buyer.

2. Each of the accused students (pleads / plead) individually before the council.

3. Anyone under the age or height limits (is / are) not permitted to enter the ride.

4. In the event that nobody (shows / show) up, we will cancel the meeting.

5. Most of the water (has / have) evaporated.

6. Everyone carrying packages (was / were) asked to walk through a metal detector.

7. None of the stores (was / were) open before 10 A.M.

8. When something breaks at home, no one ever (takes / take) the blame.

9. One of the student nurses (was / were) chosen to attend the conference in Rome.

10. Because everyone (has / have) to prove citizenship, no one (is / are) exempt from submitting a passport.

Collective nouns are usually singular.

A **collective noun** names a group of people or animals. Words like *team, faculty, class, band, committee, jury, audience, herd, flock,* and *council* are collective nouns.

> S   V
> The *flock* of geese ***flies*** south for the winter.

S   V
The *committee* ***votes*** on the issue tomorrow.

Composition Clue

Sometimes the sentence suggests that the members of the group are acting separately as individuals rather than together as a unit:

S   V
The *audience* ***were*** rattling their programs.

In such a case, a plural verb form is correct. However, using a collective noun in this way usually sounds awkward. Try recasting these awkward sentences, using a plural subject:

S   V
The *members* of the audience ***were*** rattling their programs.

PRACTICE SET 12–6

Directions: Circle the correct verb in parentheses.

Example: The city council ((appoints)/ appoint) the mayor.

1. The jury (meets / meet) in the room to the right of Courtroom A.

2. The class (leaves / leave) when the bell rings.

3. A herd of cattle (crosses / cross) the highway in the blinding snowstorm.

4. I want to be present when the band (practices / practice) the song I wrote.

5. Our team never (loses / lose) at home.

Variations in word order do not change subject/verb agreement.

In most sentences in English, the subject comes before the verb:

S   V
The *winner* of this prize ***is*** lucky.

S V
During intermission, *I* ***buy*** a drink and a snack.

In sentences in which the verb comes before the subject, the standard rules of agreement remain the same. Word order does not change agreement.

There is/there are constructions change sentence word order.

Word order changes in sentences beginning with *there is* or *there are*. In the following sentences, *there* is not the subject of the sentence.

      V   S
There **is** no *excuse* for your behavior.

      V   S
There **are** *differences* of opinion within this group.

Quick Tip

Be careful about using the contractions *here's*, *there's*, and *where's*. The *'s* stands for *is*. You create an agreement error by saying *here's the cupcakes*, *where's my shoes*, or *there's the dishes*. You must say: *Here are the cupcakes. Where are my shoes? There are the dishes.*

Questions change sentence word order.

To find the subject and verb in questions, try turning the question into a statement.

V S   S V
Is *he* a freshman?   *He* **is** a freshman.

V   S   S   V
Are *Alexis and Roberto* seniors?   *Alexis and Roberto* **are** seniors.

See Chapter 6 for more information on word order variations.

PRACTICE SET 12–7

Directions: Underline the simple subject(s) in each sentence. Then circle the correct verb in parentheses.

Example: (Was /(Were)) the tiger and the elephant in cages?

1. There (is / are) three good answers to that question.

2. (Does / Do) Maple Drive and Kennedy Boulevard intersect?

3. Where (is / are) the cards that belong with these gifts?

4. Although she had a good alibi, there (was / were) many discrepancies in her story.

5. Why (does / do) so many current movies receive "R" ratings?

Linking verbs agree with the subject, not the subject complement.

The Subject/Linking Verb/Subject Complement sentence pattern can pose a problem. Sometimes the subject is singular and the subject complement is plural, or vice versa. Consider this sentence:

S   V   SC

The funniest *part* of the play ***was*** *the mistakes.*

Some writers may be tempted to use a plural verb form to agree with the plural word *mistakes.* However, *mistakes* is not the subject. *Part* is. Because the verb must agree with *part,* the singular verb form is correct.

PRACTICE SET 12–8

Directions: Circle the correct verb in parentheses.

Example: The purpose of making two copies ((is) / are) clear.

1. His only income (is / are) his two part-time jobs.

2. Porcelain dolls (is / are) my favorite collectible.

3. The reason for her laughter (was / were) his silly jokes.

4. A bandage and a kiss (is / are) the cure for this skinned knee.

5. The most important clue in the mystery (is / are) the fingerprints.

Titles, diseases, amounts, words used as words, and gerund phrases are singular.

Many titles of works of art, such as books, poems, movies, television shows, paintings, and songs, contain plural parts, but they are singular.

Friends often *takes* place in a coffeehouse in New York.

Sunflowers is a famous painting by Van Gogh.

Although the names of diseases often end in *s*, they are singular.

Measles *is* a dangerous disease for pregnant women.

AIDS *touches* the lives of people worldwide.

Amounts of time, weight, money, and distance are usually singular.

Ten dollars *is* too much to pay for a hamburger.

Twenty-six miles *makes* a marathon.

Words or phrases used as words are always singular.

Possessions contains two sets of double letters.

"Politics makes strange bedfellows" *is* certainly true.

Gerunds used as subjects are singular, even though the phrase itself may contain plural words.

Finding my own errors *was* hard.

Pursuing your dreams *takes* diligence.

Quick Tip

Many single objects that have two parts, such as trousers, scissors, tweezers, jeans, eyeglasses, and pliers, are plural.

My jeans *are* too tight.

The pliers *grasp* the nut easily.

The phrase *the number of* is singular. The phrase *a number of* is plural.

The number of letters to answer *seems* overwhelming.

A number of people *have* already left for the convention.

PRACTICE SET 12–9

Directions: Circle the correct verb in parentheses.

Example: The clippers (needs / (need)) to be sharpened.

1. A number of mistakes (appears / appear) in the treasurer's report.

2. Watching late-night movies on television (makes / make) me sleepy.

3. His pants (is / are) so long that he keeps tripping on them.

4. Diabetes often (causes / cause) vision problems in older adults.

5. Six weeks (was / were) a long time to be away from home.

6. Keeping the files in order (requires / require) careful attention to detail.

7. Fifty dollars (seems / seem) to be what everyone is donating to the memorial fund.

8. *Cats* (is / are) a modern stage musical based on the poetry of T. S. Eliot.

9. The scissors (was / were) so dull that they hardly cut paper.

10. "Time heals all wounds" (does / do) not always prove true.

TEST YOURSELF

Directions: Circle the correct verb in parentheses.

1. Lance's major writing problem (was / were) sentence fragments.

2. There (is / are) a clarinet and a saxophone on sale at the music store at the mall.

3. Our family (celebrates / celebrate) holidays together several times a year.

4. The piano, in addition to the dining room table and chairs, (comes / come) from my grandparents' house.

5. Every computer and fax machine in the office (needs / need) to be replaced.

6. Either coffee, tea, or milk (is / are) served with dinner.

7. Everybody in the neighborhood (brings / bring) a covered dish to the block party.

8. Some of the cookies (contains / contain) chocolate chips and walnuts.

9. Knitting children's sweaters (has / have) become Ann's favorite leisure activity.

10. Bacon and eggs (appears / appear) on the breakfast menu at most restaurants.

COMPOSITION WARM-UP

Directions: Circle the correct verb in parentheses.

Example: One of the triplets ((wins) / win) every year.

1. The excuse for your three tardies (is / are) unacceptable.

2. There (is / are) thousands of people who would love to be in your place.

3. Twelve miles (is / are) a long way to travel to see a movie.

4. Either your attitude or your place of employment (is / are) going to change today.

5. Everyone in this class (is / are) expected to complete the homework.

6. Neither of the sisters (wants / want) to be on television.

7. Measles in young children (is / are) highly contagious.

8. The number of kittens in the litter (is / are) four.

9. Her salary, as well as her bonuses, (makes / make) her rich.

10. (Is / Are) there anyone who can add two plus two correctly?

11. All of the water (leaks / leak) into the pool.

12. *The Red Shoes* (is / are) a movie about ballet.

13. Every registered man and woman (has / have) the right to vote.

14. A number of questions (has / have) been answered.

15. The worst part of these meetings (is / are) the speeches.

16. Arriving on time for the games (shows / show) your interest.

17. The hamburger, in addition to the pork chops, (is / are) on the grill.

18. The raccoon and the possum (sleeps / sleep) under the bushes.

19. Somebody (has / have) taken my lunch.

20. Neither the lasagna nor the meatballs (is / are) low in calories.

COMPOSITION PRACTICE

Directions: Using all singular subjects and verbs, write five sentences on one of the following topics:

1. Finding a job
2. Raising a child
3. Surfing the Internet

Then rewrite the same paragraph, making all of your subjects and verbs plural.

WORD WATCHERS

Some words and phrases seem interchangeable, but they really are not because of the rules of grammar.

bad/badly

Bad is an adjective; *badly* is an adverb. Use *badly* to modify verbs: He sings badly.

Use *bad* to modify nouns: He is a bad singer.

Use *bad* as a subject complement: He smells bad. Do not use *bad* as an adverb (as in He sings bad), and do not use *badly* as a subject complement (as in I feel badly).

different from/different than

Different from is nearly always the correct choice. *From* is a preposition. It is followed by a noun: Baseball is different from softball.

Than is a subordinating conjunction, so it introduces a clause: Movies are different now than they used to be. It is incorrect to use *different than* before a noun (as in Baseball is different than softball.)

is when/is where/is because

These constructions are always incorrect. *Is* is a linking verb, so it must be followed by a subject complement—a noun or an adjective. *When, where,* and *because* introduce adverb clauses. Recast sentences to eliminate *is when, is where,* or *is because.*

like/as

Like is a preposition. It is followed by a noun: She looks like her mother.

As is a subordinating conjunction. It introduces a clause: I behaved as I should have.

real/really and **sure/surely**

Real and *sure* are adjectives. Use them before nouns: This is a real diamond. My bet is a sure thing.

Really and *surely* are adverbs. Use them to modify adjectives: I am really (not *real*) pleased with my new truck. He is surely sorry about forgetting her birthday.

(continued)

try to/try and   sure to/sure and

The *to* in *try to* and *sure to* is part of an infinitive: Try to behave yourself. Be sure to call me. It is incorrect to substitute *and* for *to* (as in Try and behave yourself or Be sure and call me.)

good/well

Good is an adjective, so it modifies a noun: He is a good typist.

Well is an adverb, so it modifies a verb, adjective, or adverb: He types well. It is incorrect to say, "He types good." Both can fill the subject complement position because *well* can also be an adjective meaning *healthy*. *He feels good* means he feels happy. *He feels well* means he feels healthy.

WORD WATCHERS PRACTICE SET

Directions: Choose the correct word in parentheses.

1. These directions are (different from / different than) the ones on page 26.

2. Monica plays golf as (good / well) as a pro.

3. You were late yesterday, so try (and / to) arrive on time tomorrow.

4. I really feel (bad / badly) about losing that check.

5. Love me (like / as) I love you.

6. I banged my head so (bad / badly) that I have had a headache for a week.

7. If they continue to foul the other team, they will (sure / surely) lose the game.

8. I will not go out with him because he always acts (like / as) a fool in public.

9. Zack doesn't dance very (good / well), but he is always happy to try.

10. Be sure (and / to) close the door on your way out.

Chapter 13

Pronoun Usage

Pronouns must agree with antecedents.

Now that you have learned the rules for subject/verb agreement, pronoun/antecedent agreement should not be difficult. Basically, you use the same rules to take the agreement process one step further.

Remember that an antecedent is the word a pronoun stands for. Consider the following sentences:

Jim cut *his* finger, and *he* had to get stitches.

Because the roof was leaking, the homeowner had to repair *it.*

In the first sentence, the pronouns *his* and *he* stand for the noun *Jim*—the antecedent. In the second sentence, the pronoun *it* stands for the antecedent *roof.*

Although the possessives *my, our, your, his, her, its,* and *their* function as adjectives, they are also personal pronouns and must have antecedents. Look at the following sentence.

The dog wagged *its* tail.

Its stands for the noun *dog*, the antecedent.

PRACTICE SET 13–1

Directions: In the following sentences, underline the pronouns and draw an arrow to their antecedents.

Example: President Lincoln was born in Kentucky, but he grew up in Illinois.

1. Janice felt herself blush with embarrassment.

2. The angry citizens voiced their opinions loudly at the city council meeting.

3. Tom testified that the wet conditions had contributed to his accident.

4. Mr. Tyler himself gave the welcome address.

5. Maryann left work early, but she didn't go straight home.

Pronouns agree with antecedents in number.

The most basic rule of pronoun/antecedent agreement is that the pronoun always agrees with its antecedent in number. Therefore, a singular pronoun refers to a singular antecedent, and a plural pronoun refers to a plural antecedent.

	Singular Forms	Plural Forms
First Person	I, me, my, mine, myself	we, us, our, ours, ourselves
Second Person	you, your, yours, yourself	you, your, yours, yourselves
Third Person	he, him, his, himself, she, her, hers, herself, it, its, itself	they, them, their, theirs, themselves

PRACTICE SET 13–2

Directions: In the blanks, write the appropriate pronoun from the chart above. Make sure that all pronouns agree with their antecedents.

Example: Please return the jewelry to ___its___ former location.

1. Dana and Jonathan need to return many of _____ duplicate wedding gifts.

2. Jasmine wants another chance to correct _____ research paper.

3. They prefer to return all the phone calls _____.

4. The boy _____ is responsible for the trouble he has caused.

5. Ann and Ron put the new puppy in _____ cage for the night.

Special agreement problems occur with certain pronouns.

Indefinite pronouns often cause agreement errors.

Because indefinite pronouns are nonspecific, writers often make agreement errors when using them. To help you avoid errors, study the following chart closely:

Always Singular	Always Plural	Singular or Plural
one, each, another	both	some
either, neither	few	none
everyone, everybody, everything	several	any
someone, somebody, something	many	all
anyone, anybody, anything		more
no one, nobody, nothing		most

When an indefinite pronoun is the antecedent, you must first decide if it is singular or plural and then match the pronoun form accordingly. You should ignore any prepositional phrases following indefinite pronouns that are always singular or always plural. Look at these sentences:

Incorrect: *Neither* (of the boys) passed *their* test.

Correct: *Neither* (of the boys) passed *his* test.

The singular *his* refers to the singular indefinite pronoun *neither. Boys* is not the antecedent because it is part of the prepositional phrase *of the boys*. Using the plural *their* with the singular antecedent *neither* creates an agreement error.

Consider this sentence, making sure to ignore the prepositional phrase following the singular indefinite pronoun *each:*

Each of the buildings had (*its / their*) own entrance.

Buildings cannot be the antecedent because it is part of the prepositional phrase *of the buildings*. The antecedent is the pronoun *each*, which is always singular and must take the singular *its*.

Each of the buildings had *its* own entrance.

The plural indefinite pronouns cause few problems. They sound plural and are rarely misused.

Several of the employees brought *their* children with *them* to work.

The antecedent *several* is a plural pronoun and so takes the plural pronouns *their* and *them*.

With the third group of indefinite pronouns, those that can be singular or plural, usage is more complex. Finding the antecedent for this third group contradicts the rules just discussed. Because these indefinite pronouns can be singular or plural, you must look at the rest of the sentence for a clue to determine number. This clue usually comes in the prepositional phrase that follows the indefinite pronoun.

Some of the brownies had nuts in *them.*

Some refers to the plural noun *brownies*, so use the plural pronoun *them*.

Some of the cake had nuts in *it.*

Some refers to the singular noun *cake*, so use the singular pronoun *it*.

PRACTICE SET 13–3

Directions: Write the correct pronoun in the blank. Underline its antecedent.

Example: <u>Neither</u> of the horses was in ___its___ stall.

1. Each of the mothers meets _____ children at the bus stop.

2. Many of the flowers are still in _____ original plastic containers.

3. One of the boys left _____ backpack in my car.

4. Either of the women can present _____ case to the board of directors.

5. None of the furniture is in _____ proper place.

6. None of the chairs are in _____ correct locations.

7. All of the lizards have spots on _____ tails.

8. Most of the farmland is valued for _____ fertile soil.

9. Both of the drinks had ice in _____.

10. Some of the dancers left _____ costumes in the dressing room.

Note: As a result of widespread usage, some people use the third-person plural pronouns (*they, them, their, theirs, themselves*) to refer to some singular indefinite pronouns (*everyone, everybody, someone, somebody*). This usage, acceptable in informal speech, is still considered improper in all written English and formal speech.

Informal speech: *Everyone* has the right to *their* own opinions.

All writing and formal speech: *Everyone* has the right to *his or her* own opinions.

OR

People have the right to *their* own opinions.

Trying to avoid sexist language can cause pronoun agreement errors.

Writers should avoid sexist language. Masculine pronouns (*he, him, his, himself*) once referred to gender-neutral nouns, that is, nouns that could be masculine or feminine, such as *student, doctor,* or *athlete.* Today, however, most writers choose expressions that do not discriminate.

Sexist: *Every* student should bring *his* textbook to class.

To avoid sexist writing, use plural forms when possible.

Nonsexist: *Students* should bring *their* textbooks to class.

Another option is to rephrase the sentence to avoid using a pronoun.

Nonsexist: Every student should bring *the required textbook* to class.

Some writers use the inclusive forms of *he/she, him/her, his/her,* and *himself/herself* to refer to nouns that can be masculine or feminine.

Every student should bring *his/her* textbook to class.

This practice is easy to apply to single sentences, but when you are writing a long passage, the dual form becomes repetitious. Therefore, choosing other methods of revision is preferable.

PRACTICE SET 13–4

Directions: Rewrite the following sentences, eliminating sexist language.

Example: A doctor usually has many loans to repay after he finishes medical school.

Doctors usually have many loans to repay after they finish medical school.

OR

A doctor usually has many loans to repay after finishing medical school.

1. A police officer often risks his life to protect people in his community.

2. Everyone is responsible for submitting his own tax return to the government.

3. An attorney must be honest, detail-oriented, and flexible in his dealings with clients.

4. A good nurse gives her patients comfort as well as medication.

5. Nobody appreciates what he has until he loses it.

Compound antecedents may cause agreement errors.

Compound antecedents are usually plural and, thus, take plural pronouns.

The *child and the babysitter* have returned from *their* trip to the zoo.

There are some exceptions to this rule.

1. If the compound is a unit, refer to it by a singular pronoun.

My *sister and closest friend **is*** on ***her*** way to see me.

2. If the compound nouns are preceded by the words *each* or *every*, use a singular pronoun.

Each cat and dog ***receives its*** annual license tag from the city.

3. If the compounds are joined by the correlative conjunctions *either/or, neither/nor, not only/but also* or the coordinating conjunctions *or* or *nor,* the pronoun selected refers to the antecedent closer to it.

Neither the manager nor the *salesclerks* have received *their* Christmas bonus.

Not only the elephant but also the *gorilla* is becoming extinct in *its* natural habitat.

Collective nouns usually take singular antecedents.

Collective nouns—like *team, family, committee, jury, class,* and *flock*—name a group of people or animals. These are usually considered singular and take the singular pronouns *it* and *its.*

The championship basketball *team* lost *its* final game of the regional playoffs.

If a collective noun antecedent is plural because each member of the group is acting individually, refer to it with a plural pronoun.

The *class are* busily reviewing *their* old tests for the final exam.

Because these sentences are quite awkward, though, you should try to rephrase them.

The class *members are* busily reviewing *their* old tests for the final exam.

PRACTICE SET 13–5

Directions: Write the correct pronoun form in the blanks in the following sentences.

Example: Either the jasmine or the honeysuckle will climb ___its___ trellis.

1. Each Girl Scout and troop leader must bring _____ sleeping bag to the campout.

2. The cast of the play presented long-stemmed roses to _____ director.

3. Ross and Henrietta are studying for _____ comprehensive nursing exams.

4. The leftover spaghetti and meatballs is still in _____ container in the refrigerator.

5. Neither the pencils nor the paper can be found in _____ usual spot.

6. The two families are trying _____ best to get along with each other.

7. Not only the boss but also the employees hated _____ new salary schedule.

8. Every car and truck has _____ license plate in full view.

9. The jury gave _____ decision to the judge.

10. The president and CEO of the company was rewarded for _____ community service.

Pronouns must show clear connections with antecedents.

Remember that a pronoun is a word that takes the place of a noun—its antecedent. Often, writers have problems with pronouns because they forget to make the necessary connection between the pronoun and the word or words it replaces. Sometimes writers use so many pronouns that the original antecedent becomes unclear. At other times, there is no specific antecedent at all.

The antecedent must be a noun or a noun substitute.

This, *that*, *which*, and *it* should refer to a specific antecedent, not to an entire sentence.

Incorrect: Austin volunteered to clean the garage. *This* made his parents happy.

What made his parents happy? The pronoun cannot refer to the entire sentence.

Correct: Austin volunteered to clean the garage. *This offer* made his parents happy.

Changing the vague pronoun *this* to an adjective modifying the specific noun *offer* corrects the faulty reference.

Incorrect: During President Johnson's administration, *he* initiated many social reforms.

The possessive *President Johnson's* cannot serve as the antecedent for *he* because possessives are adjectives.

Correct: During President Johnson's administration, *President Johnson* initiated many social reforms.

OR

Correct: President Johnson initiated many social reforms during his administration.

The antecedent must be clear.

Incorrect: *They* said that voting methods in Florida should be changed.

Who is *they*? Is *they* a newspaper columnist? A television reporter? A state elections supervisor? A candidate?

Correct: *An editorial in the Tampa Tribune* said that voting methods in Florida should be changed.

The antecedent must be unambiguous.

Incorrect: Janet told Andrea that *she* needs to see a therapist.

Who needs to see a therapist? Does *she* refer to Janet or Andrea? The pronoun is ambiguous.

Correct: Janet told Andrea that **Andrea** needs to see a therapist.

OR

Janet told Andrea, "I need to see a therapist."

OR

Janet told Andrea, "You need to see a therapist."

The pronoun should not be repetitious.

Incorrect: The Olympic runner *he* finished the marathon in a little over two hours.

The *he* following *Olympic runner* is unnecessary. Correct this problem by eliminating the repetitious pronoun.

Correct: The Olympic runner finished the marathon in a little over two hours.

PRACTICE SET 13–6

Directions: Correct the following sentences by eliminating unclear, ambiguous, or repetitious pronouns.

Example: They say that walking under a ladder causes bad luck.

Superstitious people say that walking under a ladder causes bad luck.

1. She had to work late, which meant that she missed the bus.

2. Dr. Smith told Jim that he needed to get more rest.

3. John Wayne he was the star of many classic Hollywood westerns.

4. In Freudian psychology, he defines the id, the ego, and the superego.

5. They say that genetics is as important as environment in determining personality.

6. I received a ticket, but it was clearly the other driver's fault.

7. Asheville it is a beautiful city in the mountains of North Carolina.

8. On the radio it said that we should get rain by the end of the week.

9. When Abigail's car was in the shop, she asked me for a ride.

10. Robert was struck by lightning while he was playing golf. This made him cautious.

Pronouns must be in the appropriate case.

Another problem area involves the case of personal pronouns. **Case** means "form." The personal pronouns have three cases, or forms: subjective, objective, and possessive. Study the chart below to familiarize yourself with these forms:

Person	Subjective	Objective	Possessive
First person (the person speaking)	I, we	me, us	my, mine, our, ours
Second person (the person spoken to)	you	you	your, yours
Third person (the person spoken about)	he, she, it, they	him, her, it, them	his, her, hers, its, their, theirs

The **subjective case** includes the pronoun forms used as subjects and subject complements.

Subject of the sentence: *We* are tired of waiting for the doctor.

Subject of a clause: Natalie is happy because *she* won the lottery.

Subject complement: It was *he* who made the announcement.

The **objective case** is used for objects of any kind—direct object, indirect object, object of a preposition.

Direct object: The detective saw *them* at the crime scene.

Indirect object: The chef gave *me* a new recipe.

Object of a preposition: At the campsite, giant ants crawled over *us*.

Possessive case forms show ownership or possession and actually function as adjectives.

The Singhs sold **their** house.

Those books are **mine.**

Usually, English speakers use the correct case forms instinctively. For instance, most speakers know to say, "I am going to a movie," not "Me am going to a movie." Several areas do cause some case problems, though.

Pronouns as subject complements must be in the subjective case.

Many speakers incorrectly use the objective case after a linking verb. For example, when answering the telephone, people make this mistake by saying, "This is him" instead of "This is he." Pronouns used as subject complements must always be in the subjective case.

Incorrect: The person who recommended the restaurant was *me*.

Correct: The person who recommended the restaurant was *I*.

Compounds often cause case errors.

Compounds may involve two or more pronouns (*she and I*) or a pronoun and a noun (*Jane and I*). To determine which pronoun case form to use, separate the compound and test it out loud. Whatever form the pronoun takes alone is the same form it takes as part of a compound.

He is going to the game. *I* am going to the game. *He and I* are going to the game.

We saw *Mary* at the mall. We saw *him* at the mall. We saw *Mary and him* at the mall.

Give the dessert to *him*. Give the dessert to *me*. Give the dessert to *him and me*.

Composition Clue

When you have two pronouns of different persons and one is first person, think about being polite, and put yourself (first person) last. Say "*him and me*," "*you and I*," "*they and we*."

Quick Tip

Many writers incorrectly use the subjective pronoun *I* in every compound involving the first person. While it is correct to say, "Robert and I left early" (subjects), it is not correct to say, "Cameron gave the package to Mike and I" (object of the preposition) or "Megan left you and I her phone number" (indirect object). One of the most frequent errors with the subjective case *I* is in the expression *between you and I*. *Between* is a preposition, so it should be followed by the objective pronoun *me*. *Between you and me* is always correct.

Comparisons with *than* or *as* require careful analysis.

When a subordinate clause uses *than* or *as* to introduce a comparison followed by a pronoun, case confusion often results. Remember that the subjective case pronouns are used as the subjects of subordinate clauses.

DC
James is smarter *than I am*.

The subject of the subordinate clause *than I am* is the subjective case pronoun *I*. To say, "James is smarter *than me am*" sounds wrong. You can also write this sentence leaving out the verb *am*. This type of clause is called an **elliptical clause** because something has been left out. Even without the verb, the subordinate clause needs a subject in the subjective case form, so you must say, "James is smarter than I," not "James is smarter than *me*."

Often, the pronoun that you choose determines the meaning of the sentence. Examine these sentences:

> He paid her more than I.

> He paid her more than me.

Which is correct? The answer depends on the writer's meaning.

> "He paid her more than *I*" means "He paid her more than I (paid her)."

> "He paid her more than *me*" means "He paid her more than (he paid) me."

The problem of determining the correct pronoun case following *than* or *as* has a simple solution: just finish the comparison, and the sound and meaning will tell you which pronoun to use.

Try this one:

> We left the party as late as (they / them).

We left the party as late as *they* did. The answer is *they*.

Appositives must maintain a consistent case.

An appositive renames the noun that it follows. A pronoun that is an appositive should be in the same case as the noun that it follows. For example, a pronoun appositive to the subject is in the subjective case, and a pronoun appositive to the direct object is in the objective case.

>   S   app.
>
> **Appositive to the subject:** The *winners* of the contest, *John and he,* received a trophy and a check.

>   DO   app.
>
> **Appositive to the direct object:** We saw two *people, Nicole and her,* sitting in the empty train station.

Note: If a pronoun comes before a noun that renames or clarifies it (*we students, us fathers*), ignore the noun, and put the pronoun in its proper case according to its use in the sentence.

> **Subject:**   *We* ~~students~~ enjoy having Fridays free.

> **Indirect object:**   The counselors gave *us* ~~fathers~~ another chance.

PRACTICE SET 13–7

Directions: Circle the correct pronoun form in parentheses.

Example: The social worker mailed (they /(them)) and (we /(us)) forms to complete.

1. His sister earned a higher grade on the English test than (he / him).

2. The neighbors and (we / us) are having a barbecue to celebrate Memorial Day.

3. The manager told James and (I / me) to come back the next day for a discount.

4. After Jenny and (she / her) arrived at the party, everyone started dancing.

5. Their friends do not ski as well as (they / them).

6. Between you and (I / me), studying every night helps a lot.

7. Please deliver the pizza to (she / her) and (he / him).

8. The winners of the contest are the Watsons and (we / us).

9. The doctor gave my brother and (I / me) a physical exam before camp.

10. The director offered a raise to two employees, Elsie and (he / him).

Pronoun case varies in verbals.

Gerunds take possessive case pronouns.

Standard English requires using the possessive case before gerunds. This is logical since gerunds are nouns and are modified by possessive adjectives.

Incorrect: The teacher resents *him* being late to class so often.

Correct: The teacher resents *his* being late to class so often.

Try this one yourself:

(I / me / my) studying every afternoon for three hours has certainly made this class easier.

The possessive *my* precedes the gerund *studying*.

My studying every afternoon for three hours has certainly made this class easier.

Pronouns before participles are in the objective case.

A pronoun that precedes a participle or a participial phrase is in the objective case.

participial phrase
We found *him stranded in the car* on a deserted highway.

Try this one:

participial phrase

The police officer saw (they / them / their) *leaving town* in a stolen car.

The objective *them* precedes the participial phrase *leaving town in a stolen car.*

The police officer saw them leaving town in a stolen car.

Pronouns before infinitives are in the objective case.

The pronoun that directly precedes an infinitive is called the **subject of the infinitive.** Because infinitives are verb forms, they can also take direct objects that receive their action. The subject and the object of an infinitive are always in the objective case.

subject of the infinitive   object of the infinitive

The mayor asked   *them*   to see   *her.*

PRACTICE SET 13–8

Directions: Circle the correct pronoun form in parentheses.

Example: I don't appreciate (you / your) following me home.

1. (They / Them / Their) turning back the clock confused everyone.

2. Can you believe (he / him / his) working overtime for so many days straight?

3. The driving instructor wanted (she / her) to concentrate on the road ahead.

4. The salesclerk saw (they / them / their) changing their clothes.

5. (I / Me / My) asking for a second helping of meatloaf pleased the chef.

6. My mother persuaded (we / us / our) to drive her to Miami for the weekend.

7. The problem is (we / us / our) staying out too late during the week.

8. (You / Your) helping me find a job has been crucial to my success.

9. His parents caught (he / him / his) talking on the phone at three in the morning.

10. The nurse discovered (I / me / my) trying to get out of bed by myself.

The ultimate case problem occurs with relative pronouns.

Like the personal pronouns, some of the relative pronouns have case forms. (See Chapter 9.)

Who and *whoever* are subjective case.

Subject of the sentence: *Who* is coming to my party?

Subject of a clause: *Whoever* parks on the grass will get a ticket.

Whom and *whomever* are objective case.

Direct object: They interviewed *whomever* the board suggested.

Object of the preposition: The child for *whom* they have been searching has been found.

In current American usage, many speakers have stopped using the pronoun *whom* altogether, but in formal speech and all writing, the case forms should be used correctly.

Whose is possessive case.

I found a wallet. *Whose* is it?

Questions beginning with relative pronouns require special attention.

To determine the case of a relative pronoun in an interrogative sentence, you must decide how the pronoun functions in the sentence—as a subject, a direct object, an object of a preposition, or a possessive.

                                          S   V

Relative pronoun as the subject: (Who / Whom) has been elected to the board of directors?

Here the pronoun is the subject of the sentence, so *who* is correct.

                                      DO   V   S   V

Relative pronoun as direct object: (Who / Whom) did the boss interview for the sales position?

Here the pronoun is the direct object, so *whom* is correct.

Quick Tip

A way to check for the correct case form of relative pronouns in questions is to answer the question with a personal pronoun. The case of your answer should be the same as the case of the relative pronoun.

Who is in charge? *She* is in charge.

She is in the subjective case, so *who* is correct.

Whom did you see? I saw *him.*

Him is in the objective case, so *whom* is correct.

Relative pronoun as object of the preposition: prep. obj. of the prep.
For (who / whom)

V S V
does the bell toll?

Here the pronoun is the object of the preposition *for*, so *whom* is correct.

Determine the case of pronouns by determining their use within noun and adjective clauses.

In complex sentences containing noun and adjective clauses, first isolate the subordinate clause. Then determine how the relative pronoun functions within the clause itself. In a subordinate clause, the relative pronoun can act as subject, subject complement, direct object, object of a preposition, or possessive adjective. How the pronoun functions in the clause determines the case. How the clause functions in the sentence is not important and has no effect on the case of the relative pronoun.

Relative pronouns may serve various functions in adjective clauses.

A relative pronoun may be the subject of an adjective clause.

┌────── adjective clause ──────┐
          S   V
The doctor *who is in charge of the clinic* trained in Australia.

To determine the subject of an adjective clause, isolate the subordinate clause (*who is in charge of the clinic*) from the rest of the sentence. Now you can see that the relative pronoun *who* is the subject of the clause, so the subjective case is correct. The subordinate clause itself is used as an adjective to modify *doctor*, but this fact has no bearing on the case of the pronoun.

A relative pronoun may be the direct object of an adjective clause.

┌────── adjective clause ──────┐
      DO   S   V
The doctor *whom we saw at the clinic* trained in Australia.

To determine the direct object of an adjective clause, isolate the adjective clause (*whom we saw at the clinic*) from the rest of the sentence. Now you can see that *we* is the subject of the clause and the relative pronoun *whom* is the direct object of the verb *saw*. Thus, the objective case form is correct.

A relative pronoun may be the object of the preposition in an adjective clause.

```
              ┌──────── adjective clause ────────┐
        prep. obj. of the prep.     S      V
  The doctor  for      whom      they waited trained in Australia.
```

To determine whether the relative pronoun is the object of the preposition in an adjective clause, isolate the adjective clause (*for whom they waited*) from the rest of the sentence. In the clause, the subject is *they*, the verb is *waited*, and *whom* is the object of a preposition (*for whom* is a prepositional phrase). Therefore, the objective case of the relative pronoun is correct.

Possessive adjectives may be used in adjective clauses.

```
              ┌──────── adjective clause ────────┐
        poss. adj.              S      V    SC
  The doctor whose surgical technique is superior trained in Australia.
```

To find the possessive adjective in an adjective clause, isolate the adjective clause (*whose surgical technique is superior*) from the rest of the sentence. In the clause, *technique* is the subject, *is* is the verb, and *superior* is a subject complement. *Whose* is a possessive adjective modifying the subject *technique*, so the possessive case is correct.

Relative pronouns may serve various functions in noun clauses.

Analyze noun clauses that begin with relative pronouns in the same way you analyze adjective clauses. Once again, how the noun clause is used in the sentence does not affect the case of the relative pronoun.

A relative pronoun may be the subject of a noun clause.

```
              ┌──────── noun clause ────────┐
               S      V
  We knew who had started the fight.
```

To find the subject of a noun clause, isolate the noun clause (*who had started the fight*) from the rest of the sentence. In this noun clause, the relative pronoun is the subject, so the subjective *who* is correct. Although the noun clause is the direct object of the verb *knew*, you do not consider this fact in determining case form.

```
               ┌─noun clause ─┐
                S       V
  I will make a picnic lunch for whoever requests it.
```

The noun clause in this sentence is *whoever requests it*. In the clause, the relative pronoun *whoever* is the subject, so the subjective case form is correct. You do *not* need to consider that the noun clause is itself the object of the preposition *for*.

A relative pronoun may be the subject complement of a noun clause.

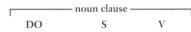

The police don't know *who the culprits are.*

To find the subject complement of a noun clause, isolate the noun clause (*who the culprits are*) from the rest of the sentence. In the noun clause, *culprits* is the subject, *are* is a linking verb, and the relative pronoun *who* is a subject complement. Thus, the subjective form *who* is correct for the pronoun as subject complement. Ignore the fact that the noun clause itself functions as the direct object of the sentence.

A relative pronoun may be the direct object of a noun clause.

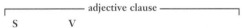

We will give a scholarship to *whomever the committee recommends.*

To find the direct object of a noun clause, isolate the clause from the rest of the sentence—*whomever the committee recommends.* When you analyze the clause, you see that *committee* is the subject, *recommends* is the verb, and the relative pronoun *whomever* is the direct object. Thus, the objective form *whomever* is correct.

Parenthetical expressions such as *they know, I think,* and *he says* are often inserted into subordinate clauses. Ignore these expressions when deciding whether to use subjective or objective case.

```
                     ┌───────────── adjective clause ─────────────┐
                       S        V
```
I met the woman *who* ~~they say~~ *is the next president of the company.*

If you eliminate the parenthetical expression *they say,* you can tell that the adjective clause is *who is the next president of the company.* Because the relative pronoun *who* is the subject of the clause, the subjective form is correct.

Other relative pronouns take special consideration.

1. Some relative pronouns do not have case forms. *That, which,* and *what* are the same in the subjective and the objective case and do not have possessive forms.

   ```
    S              O
   ```
   What matters most is *what* you do.

2. *Who, whoever, whom, whomever,* and *whose* refer to people. *Which* refers to objects and animals. *That* is appropriate for people, animals, or objects.

   The plumber *who* fixed my sink works for my brother.

   The bank, *which* usually closes at noon, will remain open until six o'clock today.

   The dog *that* barked all night annoyed my neighbor.

Quick Tip — Dropping the relative pronoun as the object of a preposition in a subordinate clause is acceptable to avoid the complications of pronoun case.

Correct: The administrator whom he worked for did not give him a bonus.

Correct: The administrator he worked for did not give him a bonus.

PRACTICE SET 13–9

Directions: Circle the correct form of the pronoun in parentheses. If there is a subordinate clause in the sentence, make sure to isolate it before making your choice.

Example: President John Kennedy, ((who) / which) was our youngest elected president, was known for his eloquent speech and keen sense of humor.

1. In the movie *Hamlet,* (who / whom) did Mel Gibson play?

2. Datacall allows counselors to talk to (whoever / whomever) needs them on campus.

3. Because the doors were locked, (whoever / whomever) was in the building couldn't leave.

4. One of the clerks (who / whom) the judge had hired left her position to work for a large law firm.

5. According to Greek myth, the Sphinx devoured those (who / whom) could not answer her riddles.

6. The editor by (who / whom) they have been criticized is preparing a formal apology.

7. (Who / Whom) is responsible for e-mailing that computer virus to so many people?

8. The raccoon (that / who / whom) lives in my yard comes out at night.

9. I will vote for (whoever / whomever) promises to reduce taxes.

10. The defendant, (who / whom) most people believed was guilty, was freed for lack of evidence.

TEST YOURSELF

Directions: Circle the correct form of the pronoun in parentheses.

1. Every giraffe and elephant on the nature preserve had a tracking device attached to (its / it's / their) ear.

2. Neither the sofa nor the recliners can be moved from (its / it's / their) present location.

3. The professional hockey team voted to extend (its / it's / their) current contract for another year.

4. The manager gave the new employee and (she / her) an excellent evaluation.

5. Everyone began arguing when Donald and (we / us) left the meeting.

6. My assistant is not as efficient as (I / me).

7. (He / Him / His) leaving town after the robbery certainly looks suspicious.

8. One of the bridesmaids left (her / their) earrings in the dressing room at the church.

9. The counselor (who / whom) they contacted about the child's behavior problems offered helpful suggestions.

10. The engineer (who / whom / which) is a consultant on the drilling project once worked in Saudi Arabia.

COMPOSITION WARM-UP

Directions: Choose the correct pronouns in the parentheses.

1. A. J. and (he / him) have requested a hearing.

2. I have no idea (who / whom) they wish to hire.

3. My father disapproves of (me / my) coming home past midnight.

4. Each of the actresses received (her / their) scripts last night.

5. We carefully laid the blanket on top of (she / her).

6. Adam and Dana invited Scott and (she / her) to their wedding.

7. (Whoever / Whomever) wrote this letter has some explaining to do.

8. I can't understand (you / your) wasting your time.

9. Neither of the boys wears (his / their) hair cut short.

10. Megan gave her old toys to Owen and (he / him).

COMPOSITION PRACTICE

1. Write a sentence using compound personal pronouns as the subjects.

2. Write a sentence containing the pronoun *whom*.

3. Write a sentence containing a possessive pronoun before a gerund.

4. Write a sentence beginning with the word *each* and containing the word *her*.

5. Write a sentence with a prepositional phrase that contains a personal pronoun as the object of the preposition.

WORD WATCHERS

The tone of your writing should depend on the assignment and the audience. Avoid overly formal or informal words and phrases.

amongst	In American English, this is an old-fashioned and pretentious way to say *among*.
firstly, secondly	These are pretentious beginnings. They begin to sound even worse as the list progresses: *fourthly, fifthly, sixthly, seventhly*. Use *first, second, third*.
male, female	*Male* and *female* are too technical when used to refer to a man and a woman unless you are writing a scientific or technical work: The man and woman (not *male and female*) sat on the bench and watched the sun set.
laid-back	This is colloquial for *casual*. You should not use any slang in your writing because not everyone will understand it; also, slang changes over time. You may not know what "gams" are (nice-looking legs) or what it means to say "It's the berries" (it's terrific!), but your great-grandfather probably does, or did.
okay	This is colloquial for *all right* or *acceptable*. Do not use it in formal writing.
didn't/can't/wouldn't	Contractions are appropriate in very informal writing, but they are out of place in formal essays.

(continued)

WORD WATCHERS PRACTICE SET

Directions: Change the inappropriate word in bold print to one that better suits the tone or eliminates the slang.

1. Her **laid-back** attitude will get her in trouble with her boss.

2. As we arrived at the basketball court, we realized that several **males** had already started to play.

3. My girlfriend says that if she won the lottery, she would divide the money **amongst** everyone at work.

4. I have several reasons for changing my mind. **Firstly,** the situation has changed.

5. You will have fifteen minutes to complete this portion of the test. Using a pencil rather than a pen is not **okay.**

6. Mario tried to explain his situation to the landlord, but the landlord just **dissed** him.

7. The **dude** in the yellow shirt is the pastor at my church.

8. The pharmacy is open **24/7.**

9. It was **my bad** that the letter was not sent in time.

10. It was **so not like him** to forget to call.

Chapter 14

Modifier Usage

Modifiers are adjectives and adverbs—including single words, phrases, or clauses—that describe another word or group of words. Modifier placement can affect the meaning of a sentence.

Place limiting modifiers—words like *just, almost, even, hardly, only, merely, nearly, simply, scarcely*, and *exactly*—next to the words they limit.

Look at the following sentence:

> Jack said that he believed me.

Now add the modifier *only*. Notice how its placement affects the meaning.

> *Only* Jack said that he believed me.

(Miguel didn't say it. Mary didn't say it. Only *Jack* said it.)

> Jack *only* said that he believed me.

(Jack didn't mean it. He only *said* it.)

> Jack said that *only* he believed me.

(Jack said that Miguel and Mary didn't believe me. Only *he* believed me.)

> Jack said that he believed *only* me.

(Jack didn't believe Miguel or Mary. He believed only *me*.)

Careless writers frequently misplace single-word modifiers that modify amounts:

Improper placement: This car *just* costs $5,000.

What word does *just* modify? This car costs $5,000, not $10,000.

Revision: This car costs *just* $5,000.

Improper placement: I *only* ran three miles today.

What word does *only* modify? I ran three miles, not five miles.

Revision: I ran *only* three miles today.

PRACTICE SET 14–1

Directions: Move misplaced modifiers in front of the words that they limit. More than one placement may be correct.

Example: They only gave us twenty minutes to finish what we were doing.

They gave us only twenty minutes to finish what we were doing.

1. When she tried to buy the groceries, she realized that she only had ten dollars in her wallet.

2. I almost sold all of the items at my garage sale.

3. The witness was not even able to identify one of the suspects.

4. They nearly refused every plan that we offered them.

5. The car lot only sells used cars.

Place single-word modifiers, modifying phrases, and modifying clauses in positions that clearly indicate what they modify.

Modifying phrases and clauses go next to or very near the words that they modify. Improper placement can cause some funny misreadings.

Improper placement: Now that they were married, she destroyed the photographs of boyfriends that she had dated reluctantly.

Did she date the boyfriends reluctantly? No, she destroyed the photographs reluctantly. Revise the sentence by putting the adverb next to what it modifies.

Revision: Now that they were married, she reluctantly destroyed the photographs of boyfriends that she had dated.

Improper placement: The Christmas lights were lovely to Janna, hanging from the tree.

Was Janna hanging from the tree? No, the Christmas lights were. Revise the sentence by putting the adjective phrase next to what it modifies.

Revision: To Janna, the Christmas lights hanging from the tree were lovely.

Improper placement: I left the box of cookies that I had baked in my car.

Did I bake the cookies in my car? No, I left them in my car.

Revision: In my car, I left the box of cookies that I had baked.

Improper placement: We all admired the room for the baby that he had painted.

Did he paint the baby? No, he painted the room.

Revision: We all admired the room that he had painted for the baby.

PRACTICE SET 14–2

Directions: Revise the following sentences, putting modifiers in the proper place.

Example: She purchased a wedding gown from a designer with a ten-foot train.

She purchased a wedding gown with a ten-foot train from a designer.

1. As she sat before the employment counselor, she calculated the number of jobs she had lost nervously.

2. The newspaper ran the story about the search for the missing documents on the front page.

3. We bought a computer program that identifies viruses at Computer City.

4. My hairdresser gave little bags to all of her clients filled with shampoo.

5. The trainer told all of the athletes to stretch before running on Tuesday.

Do not place a modifier in an unclear or confusing position.

These types of modifiers are called squinting modifiers. **Squinting modifiers** appear between two words and can modify either one. Consider this sentence:

Squinting modifier: Dining out frequently is expensive.

Does the sentence mean that it is frequently expensive to dine out, or does it mean that it is expensive to dine out frequently? Since either meaning applies, the modifier is not well placed.

Revision: Dining out is frequently expensive.

OR

It is expensive to dine out frequently.

PRACTICE SET 14–3

Directions: Revise the following sentences in two ways, eliminating squinting modifiers.

Example: The fire that was burning quickly made everyone leave the room.

The quickly burning fire made everyone leave the room.

OR

The fire that was burning made everyone leave the room quickly.

1. He knew after a year they would be married.

2. The girl I dated once starred in a Broadway show.

3. Elizabeth thought throughout the dinner the service was very slow.

4. His following my directions totally shocked me.

5. The conversation we had later settled our disagreement.

If possible, avoid putting modifiers in positions that awkwardly separate important sentence parts.

Place subjects as close as possible to verbs.

Avoid unnecessarily separating subjects from verbs.

Awkward separation: Trey, before he met his wife, was in the navy.

Revision: Before he met his wife, Trey was in the navy.

OR

Trey was in the navy before he met his wife.

Place verbs as close as possible to direct objects.

Avoid unnecessarily separating verbs from direct objects.

           S   V   DO

Awkward separation: *He asked,* before I could stop him, an embarrassing *question.*

Revision: Before I could stop him, he asked an embarrassing question.

OR

He asked an embarrassing question before I could stop him.

Keep the verbs in verb phrases together.

Avoid unnecessarily splitting auxiliary verbs from main verbs.

aux. verb   modifier   aux. verb   main verb

Awkward split: Lacey   *has   for an hour   been   proofreading* her paper.

Revision: Lacey has been proofreading her paper for an hour.

Keep the words in infinitives together.

Try to avoid splitting the *to* from the verb form of an infinitive.

infinitive   modifier   infinitive

Awkward split: He wanted   *to   carefully   address* her concerns.

Revision: He wanted to address her concerns carefully.

PRACTICE SET 14–4

Directions: Revise the following sentences for proper modifier placement.

Example: They sang, after the speeches, a patriotic song.

After the speeches, they sang a patriotic song.

1. She tried to slowly carry the vase to the table.

2. The dancer, after she regained her composure, continued with the performance.

3. He collected from everyone in the room money for the birthday present.

4. I am going to, if I can find the courage, tell her what I think.

5. The teacher was angry because the student had, during class, answered her cell phone.

Avoid dangling modifiers.

Dangling modifiers are phrases or clauses that have nothing to modify in a sentence. Consider this sentence:

Dangling modifier: *Hearing no further business,* the meeting ended.

Obviously, the meeting could not hear anything, and there is no word in the sentence for the opening phrase to modify; therefore, it is dangling.

Revision: Hearing no further business, the president ended the meeting.

Dangling modifier: *Cleaning the kitchen,* a giant cockroach scampered across the counter.

Since a cockroach can't clean a kitchen, the modifier is dangling.

Revision: Cleaning the kitchen, I saw a giant cockroach scamper across the counter.

OR

While I was cleaning the kitchen, a giant cockroach scampered across the counter.

Dangling modifier: *After brushing my teeth,* my tongue began to tingle.

Since my tongue can't brush my teeth, this modifier is dangling.

Revision: After brushing my teeth, I felt my tongue begin to tingle.

OR

While I was brushing my teeth, my tongue began to tingle.

Dangling modifier: *While driving home,* the puppy slept in the back seat.

Since the puppy can't drive home, this modifier is dangling.

Revision: While I was driving home, the puppy slept in the back seat.

PRACTICE SET 14–5

Directions: Revise the following sentences to correct dangling modifiers. Write "correct" next to any sentences that need no revision.

Example: Driving through Tampa, the orange blossoms smelled heavenly.

When I was driving through Tampa, the orange blossoms smelled heavenly.

1. Flying above the city, the people below looked like ants.

2. Cell phones should always be turned off when attending a concert.

3. While trying to study for my exam, the children playing in the street kept distracting me.

4. Quietly whispering a little prayer, the tanks drove the soldiers across the desert.

5. In order to succeed, much planning is required.

Quick Tip

Changing word order will repair misplaced modifiers, but it will not repair dangling modifiers.

Misplaced modifier: My favorite vacation photograph is the one of my grandmother as she sat atop a camel *wearing her red tennis shoes.*

Revision: My favorite vacation photograph is the one of my grandmother wearing her red tennis shoes as she sat atop a camel.

(continued)

The modifier *wearing her red tennis shoes* now appears next to *grandmother*, the word it modifies, so changing word order is effective.

Dangling modifier: *While sitting atop a camel,* my grandmother's red tennis shoes looked great.

Changing the word order in this sentence does not repair the dangling modifier.

Incorrect revision: My grandmother's red tennis shoes looked great *while sitting atop a camel.*

The red tennis shoes, not my grandmother, are still sitting atop the camel.

Revision: While sitting atop a camel, my grandmother looked great in her red tennis shoes.

The revision is correct because now my grandmother is sitting atop the camel.

PRACTICE SET 14–6

Directions: Revise these sentences containing misplaced, squinting, or dangling modifiers.

Example: While sleeping, the noisy television didn't bother Marta.

The noisy television didn't bother Marta while she was sleeping.

1. The orders he shouted quickly made the soldiers snap to attention.

2. I painted, with no one's help, three rooms in two hours.

3. This recipe only calls for four cups of flour.

4. While watching the season finale of my favorite television show, a telemarketer called.

5. Uncovering the truth, the case was closed by the detective.

6. It is important to thoroughly proofread your work.

7. The scientist was awarded his Nobel Prize wearing a golf shirt and khakis.

8. Mitch, when he wants to, can be charming.

9. Closing the car door, my skirt accidentally ripped.

10. The girl whom I see on the bus occasionally waits for me after class.

TEST YOURSELF

Directions: Revise any sentences containing misplaced, squinting, or dangling modifiers. Write "correct" next to any sentences that need no revision.

1. The victim he was comforting sadly told him what had happened.

2. Chris ate the chicken shopping at the mall.

3. Kevin, even though he hates orange juice, drinks it every morning.

4. Rover began to happily wag his tail.

5. While installing the software, a power surge destroyed the computer's operating system.

6. To understand calculus, a student must concentrate.

7. People can now get salads at fast-food restaurants who do not like hamburgers.

8. Lauren said frequently Don was late to work.

9. Climbing out of the bathtub, the washcloth fell on the floor.

10. I only buy fresh fruit.

COMPOSITION WARM-UP

Directions: Revise any sentences containing misplaced, squinting, or dangling modifiers. Write "correct" next to any sentences that need no revision.

1. The streets in my neighborhood, whenever it rains, flood.

2. I only paid fifty dollars for that lamp.

3. Singing in the shower, the soap splashed into my eyes.

4. Madison asked me to, when I could, call her to arrange a meeting.

5. Angry with his parents, the bedroom seemed like a good place to cool off.

6. Being a fan of the rock group, the concert tickets seemed inexpensive.

7. Act II of the play just has two scenes.

8. The pianist played the song for the class using his sheet music.

9. Hungry for his supper, the dog rattled his bowl.

10. While driving down Main Street, the stoplights were out of order.

COMPOSITION PRACTICE

Directions: Rewrite the following paragraph, correcting any misplaced or dangling modifiers.

Today started out in the worst way. First, I set my alarm clock for 6:00 P.M. instead of 6:00 A.M. Waking up at 7:30 A.M., my day was already off to a bad start. Before taking a shower, my boss had to be called to report that I would be coming in late for work. I was ready to finally leave when I discovered that my key ring was missing. My car keys had to be found before leaving the house. They neither were in my briefcase nor in my pants pocket. Suddenly looking under the couch, there they were. Quickly I wrapped a Pop Tart in aluminum foil from the toaster and ran out the door. My bad luck got worse. My car would not start. Being dead, I thought that I would have to buy a new battery, but my kind neighbor was able to use cables to jump-start my car. When at last arriving at work, everyone cheered.

WORD WATCHERS

Weak words and clichés are so overused that they have become meaningless. Avoid these expressions in your writing:

nice	dead as a doornail
fun	bored to death
interesting	quiet as a mouse
thing	happily ever after

(continued)

WORD WATCHERS PRACTICE SET

Directions: Rewrite the following sentences, replacing the boldfaced clichés or weak words with meaningful language.

1. I let her go ahead of me in line because **what goes around comes around.**

2. I put all of my **stuff** in the locker and then left for class.

3. I think I did well on the test, **but time will tell.**

4. She doesn't have enough money to buy that house, but if she keeps saving, **someday her ship will come in.**

5. I finally agreed to let my children watch television on school nights **because if you can't beat them, join them.**

6. She thinks she can move in with him without repercussions, but **there is no such thing as a free lunch.**

7. The party was **fun,** but Ruben looked **bored to death.**

8. He shouldn't worry about losing his job because **every cloud has a silver lining.**

9. When you are trying to lose weight, it is important to **take it one step at a time.**

10. Many people who have tried to find partners on the Internet have learned that **beauty is only skin deep.**

Chapter 15

Sentence Coherence: Logic, Parallelism, and Shifts

Sentence coherence creates clear sentences.

Coherent sentences—sentences that make sense—result when writers use the appropriate parts of speech in the various sentence parts.

Subjects are usually nouns, pronouns, or forms of nouns like gerunds or noun clauses.

The *dogs* barked loudly. (subject–noun)

Loud barking annoys me. (subject–gerund)

That the dogs barked loudly was the main complaint. (subject–noun clause)

Complements are nouns, pronouns, forms of nouns, or adjectives.

The house was really a *mansion.* (subject complement–noun)

A mansion was *what we really wanted.* (subject complement–noun clause)

The structure of the mansion was *unstable.* (subject complement–adjective)

The comment made me *angry.* (object complement–adjective)

Adverbs, adverb phrases, and adverb clauses modify verbs, adjectives, or other adverbs.

```
        ┌────── adverb phrase ──────┐
    prep.  gerund   obj. of a prep.
     By    studying      hard, I know I will pass the state board exam.
```

The introductory adverb phrase in this sentence modifies the verb *will pass.*

Faulty sentences use incorrect parts of speech.

Do not use a prepositional phrase as the subject.

adv. phrase   pred.

Incorrect: *By following the map will get* you there quickly.

In this example, a prepositional phrase incorrectly serves as the subject of the sentence, creating a mixed construction. There are several ways to correct this sentence.

1. Drop the preposition *by,* leaving a gerund phrase as the subject.

S   pred.

Following the map will help you get there quickly.

2. Add a noun or pronoun as the subject.

adv. phrase   S   pred.

By following a map, you will get there quickly.

3. Recast the sentence.

S   adj. clause   pred.

Those who follow the map will get there quickly.

Do not use an object of a preposition as the subject.

prep.   O   pred.

Incorrect: *In* Tom Sawyer *gets* his friends to whitewash his fence.

In this sentence, *Tom Sawyer* is the object of the preposition *in,* so *Tom Sawyer* cannot serve as the subject.

You can correct this sentence by adding a subject.

prep.   O   S pred.

Correct: *In* Tom Sawyer, *Tom gets* his friends to whitewash his fence.

Do not use an adverb clause as the subject.

adv. clause   pred.

Incorrect: *Just because she has a cold does* not *mean* that she will miss class.

In this example, an adverb clause incorrectly serves as the subject. You can correct this sentence in several ways:

1. Change the adverb clause to a gerund phrase.

gerund phrase   pred.

Her having a cold does not *mean* that she will miss class.

2. Add a pronoun subject.

adv. clause   S   pred.

Just because she has a cold, she will not necessarily *miss* class.

3. Recast the sentence.

She has a cold, but she will not miss class.

PRACTICE SET 15–1

Directions: Rewrite the following sentences, correcting the mixed constructions.

Example: Whenever I follow my instincts gets me in trouble.

Following my instincts gets me in trouble.

OR

Whenever I follow my instincts, I get in trouble.

1. Because the truck has a dead battery means I need a jump-start.

2. By asking for directions will make me look lost.

3. Even though she had flu shots doesn't mean she will not get sick on her vacation.

4. In Shakespeare's *Hamlet* does not know whether to live or die.

5. After losing my wallet caused me much inconvenience.

Sentences are faulty when the wrong part of speech begins the predicate.

Avoid *is where*, *is when*, and *is because* constructions.

Remember that subject complements follow linking verbs. Subject complements are always nouns, pronouns, or adjectives, never adverbs. A mixed construction occurs when an adverb clause directly follows linking verbs such as *is/are*, *was/were*, especially in definitions or explanations.

	S	linking verb	adv. clause SC
Incorrect:	A metaphor	is	where a writer makes a direct comparison.

	S	linking verb	adv. clause SC
Incorrect:	A lunar eclipse	is	when the moon enters the earth's shadow.

Avoid sentences using *is when* or *is where*. You can correct these sentences by recasting them, eliminating the adverb clause after *is*.

Correct: A metaphor is a direct comparison that a writer makes.

Sometimes, you can keep the adverb clause by changing the verb from a linking verb to an action verb.

Correct: A lunar eclipse occurs when the moon enters the earth's shadow.

Another troublesome construction of this type occurs with the words *reason is because.*

<pre>
                                                        adv. clause
              S   linking verb   SC
Incorrect: The reason for our being late   is   because we missed the bus.
</pre>

This sentence has an adverb clause after the linking verb *is.* In addition, the words *reason/because* and *reason/why* are similar in meaning and should not be used together. You can correct this sentence by doing the following:

1. Change the adverb clause to a noun clause:

    The reason for our being late is that we missed the bus.

2. Recast the sentence to avoid wordiness:

    We are late because we missed the bus.

Sentences are faulty when the subjects and predicates do not logically connect.

Sentences are faulty when the subjects and predicates do not make sense together.

<pre>
             S   pred.
Incorrect: The decision to take a cruise would be fun for everyone.
</pre>

This sentence is not logical. The decision would not be fun—the cruise would. Correct the sentence by using a subject and predicate that make sense.

Correct: Taking a cruise would be fun for everyone.

PRACTICE SET 15–2

Directions: Rewrite the following sentences, correcting predicate errors.

Example: The reason that the floor was so expensive was because the tiles were made in Italy.

The floor was so expensive because the tiles were made in Italy.

1. Aerobics is when a person exercises for an extended period at a high heart rate.

2. The purchase of a DVD player produced a super-sharp picture.

3. The reason that the car crashed was because the brakes were faulty.

4. The lecture method is the kind of professor that I prefer.

5. A storm surge is where high tides cause flooding.

Sentences are faulty when they make illogical comparisons.

Do not leave out the word *other* in comparisons.

Comparisons are faulty when writers leave out necessary words in the comparison form. Sometimes the word *other* is needed to make a comparison logical. Examine this sentence:

Confusing: Jupiter is larger than any planet orbiting the sun.

Obviously, the writer means that Jupiter is the largest of the planets that orbit the sun. The sentence, however, says that Jupiter is *larger* than any of those planets. Since Jupiter *is* one of those planets, the sentence suggests that Jupiter is larger than itself. You can correct this problem by adding the word *other:*

Correct: Jupiter is larger than any *other* planet orbiting the sun.

Do not create two meanings with *than* or *as*.

Comparisons using the words *than* and *as* must be complete to avoid confusion. Here is a sentence that has two possible meanings:

Confusing: Gwen treated Bob better than his friend.

Did Gwen treat Bob better than she treated his friend, or did Gwen treat Bob better than his friend treated Bob? You must add additional information to clarify the meaning.

Correct: Gwen treated Bob better than she treated his friend.

OR

Gwen treated Bob better than his friend did.

Do not leave out *as*.

Sometimes writers leave out the word *as* when it is part of the comparison form. Examine this sentence:

Confusing: The play is as long if not longer than the movie.

The comparison forms in this sentence are *as long as* and *longer than*. All parts of both forms must be included.

Correct: The play is as long as if not longer than the movie.

PRACTICE SET 15–3

Directions: Rewrite the following sentences, making the comparisons clear and complete.

Example: The director criticized the actor more than the producer.

The director criticized the actor more than she criticized the producer.

OR

The director criticized the actor more than the producer did.

1. The green apple is as sweet if not sweeter than the red one.

2. The newly designed car seat at Babytown is more expensive than any car seat on the market.

3. Maggie was more afraid of the iguana than Matt.

4. This chocolate cake is better than any cake I have ever tasted.

5. His comments were as honest if not more honest than I expected them to be.

Parallelism creates balanced sentences.

Parallelism—using the same form of words, phrases, or clauses for items that appear together—helps make writing consistent and logical. Compare the following two sentences:

Incorrect: I have always enjoyed *reading about composers, to listen to symphonies,* and *then I go to concerts.*

Correct: I have always enjoyed *reading about composers, listening to symphonies, and going to concerts.*

In the first sentence, three groups of words appear together, but they are not parallel. *Reading, to listen,* and *I go* are three different grammatical forms: a gerund, an infinitive, and a clause. The second example uses three gerunds, *reading, listening,* and *going,* each followed by a prepositional phrase. These items are parallel in structure.

Words, phrases, and clauses joined by coordinating conjunctions (*and, but, or, for, nor, so, yet*) should be parallel.

Parallel words: I try to avoid any activity that involves *diving* or *climbing.*

Parallel phrases: The squirrel ran *in the flower beds, around the benches,* and *over the statues.*

Parallel clauses: You should study for the test with someone *who has taken good notes, who has taped the lectures,* or *who has maintained a high grade point average.*

Pairs of words, phrases, and clauses used with correlative conjunctions (*either/or, neither/nor, both/and, not only/but also*) should be parallel.

Parallel words: She told the guests to bring not only *vegetables* but also *desserts* to the party.

Parallel phrases: My watch is either *in the car* or *on my dresser.*

Parallel clauses: Sydney always revealed not only *what she thought* but also *what all of her friends thought.*

Parallel constructions should be complete.

In parallel constructions, be careful not to leave out words that are necessary to complete the meaning. Examine the following sentence:

Incorrect: The soprano *never has* and *never will* sing rock music.

The two helping verbs, *has* and *will*, signal a change in verb tense, one past perfect and one future, so they cannot "share" the main verb *sing*. *Has* requires the past participle *sung*.

Correct: The soprano never has sung and never will sing rock music.

Incomplete parallelism also occurs with prepositions. Specific prepositions follow certain verbs in English, creating particular meanings. These expressions are **idioms,** word combinations peculiar to the language. For example, *waited **on,** waited for,* and *waited **with*** all have distinct meanings. Examine the following sentence:

Incorrect: He capitalized and invested in the booming stock market.

The verbs *capitalized* and *invested* cannot "share" the preposition *in* because the idiom is *capitalize on,* not *capitalize in.* The sentence should say:

Correct: He capitalized *on* and invested *in* the booming stock market.

PRACTICE SET 15–4

Directions: Rewrite the following sentences, correcting any faulty parallelism.

Examples:

I like to exercise in the morning, before lunch, and when it is evening.

I like to exercise in the morning, before lunch, and in the evening.

He appealed and relied on the committee for his support.

He appealed to and relied on the committee for his support.

1. Are you here to apply for a job, buy something, or do you want to enroll in a cooking class?

2. My favorite ways to relax are to take a drive in the country, working out at the spa, and then watch an old movie.

3. Being late for work, forgetting to wear your identification badge, and too many coffee breaks will get you fired.

4. You should pursue either a career in nursing or become a teacher.

5. The teacher has always tried to be fair in his grading practices, suggest a number of ways to improve, and always having very organized lessons.

Avoiding shifts makes sentences consistent.

Consistency avoids confusion and makes writing flow smoothly. Awkward shifts occur when writers change point of view, voice, verb tense, or expression within a sentence.

Maintain a consistent point of view throughout a sentence.

Changing pronouns, sometimes called **shifting point of view,** causes writing to become unclear and awkward.

- **First-person point of view** uses the pronouns *I* and *we.* Use first-person point of view for informal writing in letters, personal stories, or autobiographical essays.

- **Second-person point of view** uses the pronoun *you.* Use second-person point of view for instruction and commands.

- **Third-person point of view** uses the pronouns *he, she, it,* and *they.* Many writers reserve the third person for formal writing in essays and other research projects.

A problem occurs when writers unintentionally change persons in the middle of writing. Examine the following sentence:

Shift in point of view: *Contestants* have a good chance of winning if *you* start practicing a year in advance.

Contestants is the third person. In the next part of the sentence, however, the second-person pronoun *you* refers to this same third-person word—*contestants.* The sentence contains a shift in person. To correct this problem, make the pronouns consistent:

Third-person point of view: *Contestants* have a good chance of winning if *they* start practicing a year in advance.

Second-person point of view: *You* have a good chance of winning if *you* start practicing a year in advance.

PRACTICE SET 15–5

Directions: Rewrite the following sentences, correcting any shifts in person.

Example: Before a student gives a speech, you should rehearse it before a mirror.

Before you give a speech, you should rehearse it before a mirror.

1. Workers must file for compensation early, if you expect to get paid this year.

2. She has always considered one's appearance her best asset.

3. I always leave early on Friday afternoons even when I know you shouldn't.

4. A person never really knows when you will be called on to give one's opinion.

5. Parents should always bear in mind your child's feelings about separation.

Maintain a consistent voice within a sentence.

In a sentence written in the active voice, the subject does the acting:

S V
I hit the ball.

In a sentence written in the passive voice, the action *happens* to the subject:

S   V
The *ball was hit* by me.

Keeping the voice consistent is important. Examine the following sentence:

active voice
Voice shift: He *made* plans with some friends to go to the beach, and then he

passive voice
was asked by his boss to report to work.

The first part of the sentence is written in the active voice. The subject, *he*, does the action, *made plans*. The second part of the sentence shifts to the passive voice. The subject doesn't act; something *happens* to him. The subject *he* was asked by his boss.

active voice

Correct: He *made* plans with some friends to go to the beach, and then his boss

active voice

asked him to report to work.

PRACTICE SET 15–6

Directions: Rewrite the following sentences, making the voice consistent in each one.

Example: When the family took their vacation to Israel, their dreams were fulfilled.

The family fulfilled their dreams when they took their trip to Israel.

1. After I finished ironing the last blouse, I was given two more wrinkled shirts by my sister.

2. Whenever I see the doctor, I am always told that I am in good health.

3. The technician tested our TV set and was instructed by my father to make the necessary repairs.

4. She poured the batter into the cake pan, and the pan was then placed into the oven.

5. When the escaped convict was caught by the police, they put him in handcuffs.

Maintain consistent and clear verb tenses within a sentence.

Writers sometimes change tenses to show natural progression of time.

present tense   future tense

After I *go* to the bank, I *will go* to the store.

In this sentence, the tense changes logically from present to future. A problem occurs when writers start a sentence in one tense and illogically shift to another:

present tense   past tense

Tense shift: He *walks* outside and *left* the door open.

In the following sentences, the tenses are consistent:

present tense   present tense

Correct: He *walks* outside and *leaves* the door open.

past tense   past tense

Correct: He *walked* outside and *left* the door open.

PRACTICE SET 15–7

Directions: Rewrite the following sentences, correcting any illogical shifts in verb tense.

Example: I offered him a chair and sit beside him.

I offer him a chair and sit beside him.

OR

I offered him a chair and sat beside him.

1. One night last summer, we walked on the golf course and watch the meteor shower.

2. When I suddenly came upon a hummingbird, it flies away.

3. In March, Gary decides to give her a ring and married her in April.

4. The child was happy with her grade, but her mother is not pleased.

5. She picked flowers from her garden and gives them to her lonely neighbor.

Do not mix styles of expression by changing from direct quotations to indirect quotations.

A direct quotation repeats someone's exact words.

Mary asked, "Will you go with me to the aquarium?"

An indirect quotation gives the same information without using someone's exact words:

Mary asked if I would go with her to the aquarium.

Both of these methods of expression are correct. Mixing them, however, is very confusing and awkward, especially in the same sentence.

Mixed expression: Mary asked would I like to go with her to the aquarium.

Often sentences using mixed expression sound as if they contain a question in the middle of a statement. To correct this problem, choose either direct quotation or indirect quotation.

Indirect quotation: Mary asked whether I would like to go with her to the aquarium.

OR

Direct quotation: Mary asked, "Would you like to go with me to the aquarium?"

PRACTICE SET 15–8

Directions: Rewrite the following sentences, correcting any shifts in expression.

Example: I wondered if she should go or should she stay.

I wondered if she should go or stay.

OR

I wondered, "Should she go, or should she stay?"

1. After the game, we tried to decide did we want to go to a movie.

2. John asked if I had the answers to the questions and could he borrow them.

3. The entomologists don't know whether the strange insect can protect itself or will it become extinct.

4. Please let me know if you can come over and will you bring your CDs.

5. The teacher told the class not to talk when she left the room and would the students please stay in their seats.

TEST YOURSELF

Directions: Rewrite the following sentences, correcting errors in sentence continuity, parallelism, and shifts.

1. When one has a cold, you should drink plenty of fluids.

2. He ate everything in sight and then says he is still hungry.

3. By eating oatmeal will lower your cholesterol.

4. The coach said that he was finished and did anyone have any questions.

5. He is as funny if not funnier than David Letterman.

6. Eating properly, exercising consistently, and sleep are three requirements of good health.

7. Just because you can't swim, doesn't mean we can't go to the beach.

8. The reason he impressed her is because he is a doctor.

9. In order to make the soup, a chicken was placed in the pot by Jessica.

10. Her buying an expensive fabric made beautiful curtains.

COMPOSITION WARM-UP

Directions: Rewrite the following sentences, correcting errors in sentence continuity, parellelism, and shifts.

1. The quarterback is more likely to be injured than any player on the team.

2. He picked up the phone, and then the number was dialed with care.

3. Although you need a haircut doesn't mean you will look funny in the photograph.

4. A grand slam is when a batter hits a home run when the bases are loaded.

5. You forgot to give me my allowance is why I don't have any money.

6. My hair stylist asked did I want my hair highlighted.

7. MacKenzie is either lying, or Sammie has her facts wrong.

8. I won't go to a movie theater where you can't buy popcorn.

9. I told Max the answer before Tom.

10. The height of the grass was hard to mow.

COMPOSITION PRACTICE

Write eight sentences on how to behave upon meeting a boyfriend's or girlfriend's parents for the first time. Show parallelism at least once, use consistent tense and person throughout each sentence, and make logical connections. Do not use passive voice.

WORD WATCHERS

Be sure that your writing does not include inappropriate or offensive language.

sexist language	Most words can be written as gender-neutral: waiter/waitress = server

(continued)

WORD WATCHERS
(cont.)

	mankind = humankind
	fireman = firefighter
	mailman = postal worker or letter carrier
	steward/stewardess = flight attendant

obscenities and vulgar language   It is never appropriate to use language that can be offensive to your readers. Offensive words that have become part of your everyday vocabulary may not be suitable for an essay. If you are unsure, leave them out.

name calling   Do not use derogatory terms to refer to people. These include obviously offensive terms that you would not use in polite company, but they also include words that categorize or stereotype. Be careful about using impolite terms like *jerk* or *cripple*.

WORD WATCHERS PRACTICE SET

Directions: In the following sentences, replace sexist language with gender-neutral terms.

1. The waiter forgot to bring the catsup but remembered the napkins.

2. Each voter should bring his registration card.

3. I really admire firemen because they put their lives on the line every day.

4. The discovery of penicillin has been important for all of mankind.

5. Airline stewardesses do more than just serve drinks to passengers.

6. All businessmen should take courses in management so they will know how to deal with people.

7. All department chairmen should report to the dean before Tuesday.

8. We will invite all of the doctors and their wives to the conference.

9. Because I love animals, I wear only clothes sewn with manmade fabrics.

10. I really appreciate the workmanship of the craftsmen who made this table.

Chapter 16

Parts of Speech: Reference and Review

The study of grammar includes classifying or sorting words into categories called parts of speech. To determine the part of speech of a word, you must examine it within the context of the sentence because so many words in English can function as more than one part of speech. Take the word *dream*, for example.

I often *dream* about faraway places.

(In this sentence, the word *dream* is a verb. I do what? I *dream*.)

The *dream* scene in the movie created an eerie background to the action.

(Here *dream* is an adjective. What kind of scene? A *dream* scene.)

Follow your *dream*.

(In this example, *dream* is a noun, the direct object of the verb *follow*. Follow what? Follow your *dream*.)

Words can be nouns, pronouns, verbs, adjectives, adverbs, conjunctions, prepositions, or interjections.

Verbs express action or condition.

As the main word or words in the predicate, verbs are necessary to make a complete sentence. The forms of verbs change, depending on time, mood, voice, person, and number.

Verbs have three principal parts that create all of the tenses.

1. Basic form

The **basic form** is the one that you find in the dictionary. It is really the infinitive form (*to* plus the verb) without the *to*, so that *to dance* becomes simply the basic form *dance*.

We *dance* at the club on Friday night.

2. **Past tense form**

The second principal part of a verb, in this case *danced*, is the simple **past tense,** with no helping verbs.

We *danced* at the club last week.

3. **Past participle form**

The **past participle** combines with helping verbs to create certain tenses. For most regular English verbs, the past tense and the past participial forms are the same.

We *have danced* at the club every Friday for the past two months.

Two other secondary forms do not usually appear in typical verb lists. First is the **-s form,** which is used for third person singular, and second is the **-ing form,** or **present participle.**

Verbs may be regular or irregular in form.

Regular verbs form the past and past participle by adding -*d* or -*ed* to the basic form.

Basic	Past Tense	Past Participle
learn	learned	learned
mow	mowed	mowed
bake	baked	baked

Irregular verbs do not follow the regular -*d* or -*ed* pattern in the past tense. They form their past and past participle by changing some or all of their forms (*become/ became/become; eat/ate/eaten*) or by not changing at all (*put/put/put*).

The following chart shows some common irregular verbs.

Basic	Past Tense	Past Participle
arise	arose	arisen
be	was/were	been
become	became	become
begin	began	begun
bleed	bled	bled
blow	blew	blown
break	broke	broken
bring	brought	brought
build	built	built
burst	burst	burst
buy	bought	bought
catch	caught	caught
choose	chose	chosen
come	came	come
dig	dug	dug
draw	drew	drawn
drink	drank	drunk

Basic	Past Tense	Past Participle
drive	drove	driven
eat	ate	eaten
feel	felt	felt
fight	fought	fought
find	found	found
fly	flew	flown
forget	forgot	forgotten
freeze	froze	frozen
get	got	gotten
give	gave	given
go	went	gone
have	had	had
hide	hid	hidden
hit	hit	hit
hurt	hurt	hurt
know	knew	known
lay	laid	laid
lead	led	led
lie	lay	lain
lose	lost	lost
make	made	made
pay	paid	paid
quit	quit	quit
read	read	read
ride	rode	ridden
ring	rang	rung
run	ran	run
see	saw	seen
set	set	set
shine	shone	shone
shrink	shrank	shrunk
sing	sang	sung
sit	sat	sat
slide	slid	slid
speak	spoke	spoken
spring	sprang	sprung
stink	stank	stunk
swim	swam	swum
swing	swung	swung
take	took	taken
teach	taught	taught
throw	threw	thrown
wear	wore	worn
write	wrote	written

Verbs are either action, linking, or helping.

Action verbs show some kind of activity.

I *think* before I *speak.*

The batter *popped* the ball into center field.

Samuel *waited* for the rain to stop before he *left* the building.

Action verbs are transitive or intransitive. **Transitive verbs** take direct objects, which receive the action of the verb.

   S   TV   DO
She called the repairman after the storm.

   S   TV   DO
The pilot started the engine.

Intransitive verbs do not take direct objects; the action is complete without a word in the predicate to receive the action.

                        S   IV
Forgetting to bring his sweatshirt, Marcus shivered in the freezing wind.

                        S   IV
Under the shade of an umbrella, we read by the pool.

Linking verbs connect a word in the predicate with the subject.

Linking verbs connect the subject to a subject complement, which is a noun, pronoun, or adjective in the predicate that renames or describes the subject. Linking verbs include the following:

1. All forms of *be* (*am, is, are, was, were, be, being, been*)
2. Verbs of the five senses (*feel, smell, taste, look,* and *sound*)
3. Other verbs like *appear, seem, become, grow*

                            S   linking verb   SC (adj.)
After the long interview, the applicant   *appeared*   tired.

In this sentence, the linking verb *appeared* connects *tired* to *applicant.* There is no direct object that receives any action, but there is a word—the subject complement *tired*—that describes the subject.

        S   linking verb SC (noun)
Joseph Farmington   *was*   captain   of the team for ten months.

Here the linking verb connects *captain* to *Joseph Farmington,* renaming the subject. The same verb can be a linking verb or an action verb.

     S   action verb   DO
He   *tasted* the flavored coffee.

In this sentence the subject is actually doing the action of tasting.

          S   linking verb   SC (adj.)
    The coffee   *tasted*   bitter.

Here the verb does not show action. It states a condition. It links the adjective *bitter* to the subject *coffee*.

PRACTICE SET 16–1

Directions: In the sentences below, underline the verb twice. In the first blank, identify the verb as transitive, intransitive, or linking. In the second blank, write the direct object or subject complement if there is one.

Example: He is a very good reader.   linking   reader

1. A boy from India solved the difficult problem.   _____   _____

2. Many graduates tossed their caps in the air.   _____   _____

3. Austin applauded at the end of the long song.   _____   _____

4. The sky grew dark with the approaching storm clouds.   _____   _____

5. I sounded the whistle at the beginning of the race.   _____   _____

6. The horn sounded loud in the quiet evening.   _____   _____

7. Working later than usual, he finished at midnight.   _____   _____

8. Simon planted the trees by the new fence.   _____   _____

9. Time is money.   _____   _____

10. Lightning struck the tall steeple of the old church.   _____   _____

Helping verbs combine with main verbs to form verb phrases.

Helping verbs are also called **auxiliary verbs.** They combine with *-ing* verb forms and past participle verb forms to make verb phrases. The following verbs can also appear as main verbs:

    does, do, did   *has, have, had*   *am, is, are, was, were, be, being, been*

Helping verbs also include **modals**—*will, would, shall, should, can, could, may, might, must.* Modals never appear alone as main verbs.

      helping verb main verb   helping verb main verb
    I   have   visited the dentist many times, but I   must   go   again soon.

Verbs have tenses that show the time of the action or condition.

The English language has three basic tenses.

1. Present tense

The **present tense,** which uses the first principal part of the verb, indicates a current condition, present action, repeated action, or habitual action.

> You *are* hungry.
>
> He *sings* for his supper.
>
> I *walk* every day.
>
> Dogs *bark* at the moon.

2. Past tense

The **past tense,** which uses the second principal part of the verb, indicates that something has already occurred and is now finished.

> You *were* hungry.
>
> He *sang* for his supper.
>
> I *walked* every day last week.

3. Future tense

The **future tense** indicates that something will happen. The future tense uses the first principal part of the verb plus the helping verb *will*.

> You *will be* hungry.
>
> He *will sing* for his supper.
>
> I *will walk* every day next week.

In addition to the three basic tenses, English uses three **perfect tenses** to show the relationship of times within a sentence.

1. Present perfect tense

The **present perfect tense** indicates an action that has started in the past and either is still going on or has been completed by the present time. To form the present perfect tense, use the auxiliary verb *has* or *have* plus the past participle of the main verb.

> Over the years, I *have found* many rare shells along the beach.
>
> He *has made* four calls to the cable company since yesterday.

2. Past perfect tense

The **past perfect tense** indicates that one action in the past was completed before another past action. To form the past perfect tense, use the auxiliary verb *had* plus the past participle of the main verb.

Hannah used crutches because she *had broken* her ankle in a skiing accident.

Neal *had* already *eaten* dinner by the time his mother arrived with the pizza.

3. Future perfect tense

The **future perfect tense** indicates an action that will be completed before a certain time in the future. To form the future perfect tense, use the auxiliary form *will have* plus the past participle of the main verb.

We *will have worked* a total of sixty hours by the time the project is finished.

By tomorrow, the sled dogs *will have crossed* the finish line.

The basic tenses and the perfect tenses have corresponding **progressive tenses** to indicate action that is continuing in the past, present, or future. Form the progressive tenses by combining the appropriate tense of the verb *be* with a present participle.

Present progressive: I *am staying* for the second act.

Past progressive: You *were working* at the same store ten years ago.

Future progressive: He *will be standing* for the entire ceremony.

Present perfect progressive: They *have been signing* autographs for hours.

Past perfect progressive: Everyone *had been studying* very hard.

Future perfect progressive: By noon today, we *will have been rehearsing* for three days.

PRACTICE SET 16–2

Directions: In the following sentences, underline the verbs or verb phrases twice, and indicate the tense of each.

Example: I was running the race.   *past progressive*

1. He is walking away from the accident.   _____

2. The wind whistled.   _____

3. We will have been driving for eight hours.   _____

4. He had received his mail before noon.   _____

5. The horse runs freely in the field.   _____

6. I will call you in the morning.   _____

7. The neighbor's dog had hurt the pet rabbit.   _____

8. We will spend our vacation in Hawaii.   _____

9. You have read that book more than once.   _____

10. The deer run when they hear the footsteps

_____

of a human.

_____

Verbs indicate mood.

Verbs occur in three moods: indicative, imperative, and subjunctive.

1. **Indicative mood**

   The **indicative mood** expresses statements of facts or questions.

   The U.S. government includes the legislative, executive, and judicial branches.

   What is the longest river in the world?

2. **Imperative mood**

   The **imperative mood** expresses direct requests or commands.

   Feed the dog, and take out the garbage.

3. **Subjunctive mood**

   The **subjunctive mood** expresses wishes, conditions contrary to fact, and requests and commands.

Wish:	I wish I were sitting in the bleachers at the Daytona 500.
Indicative mood:	I *was* sitting in the bleachers.
Subjunctive mood:	I wish I *were* sitting in the bleachers.
Condition contrary to fact:	If he were a good swimmer, he could finish the race.
Indicative mood:	He *was* a good swimmer.
Subjunctive mood:	If he *were* a good swimmer, . . .
Requests and commands:	She demanded that they be present.
	She requested that he remain quiet.
Indicative mood:	They are present.
	He remains quiet.
Subjunctive mood:	She demanded that they be present.
	She requested that he remain quiet.

Quick Tip

There are no *s* endings in the subjunctive mood. Notice that *to be* in the subjunctive mood is always *were*, regardless of the subject:

I wish *I were,* I wish *you were,* I wish *he were,* I wish *they were*

if *I were,* if *you were,* if *he were,* if *they were*

PRACTICE SET 16–3

Directions: Rewrite the following sentences, correcting any errors in mood.

Example: If I was the leader, we would not cross the rapids on a raft.

If I were the leader, we would not cross the rapids on a raft.

1. I wish Gavin Langwell was my trainer.

2. The store requested that he brings his copy of the guarantee.

3. If he was my brother, I would advise him not to go.

4. Sandy insisted that her friend is added to the eligibility list.

5. Serena wishes she was taller.

Verbs may be in active or passive voice.

Active voice indicates that the subject of the sentence is doing the action.

The mice ate the cheese.

The children tease the dog.

Mr. Wilson has painted his house several times.

Passive voice indicates that the subject receives the action of the verb.

The cheese was eaten by the mice.

The dog was teased by the children.

The house was painted several times by Mr. Wilson.

Quick Tip

The preposition *by* frequently indicates the passive relationship between the actor and the receiver of the action.

As the captain descended the stairs, he was welcomed *by* a large crowd.

The general was supported *by* his troops.

Composition Clue

Overusing the passive voice creates wordy and weak writing, so use it sparingly. However, on occasion, you can use the passive voice for variety or to emphasize the receiver of the action rather than the actor.

Passive voice: The frightened deer was hit by the car. (This sentence emphasizes the deer.)

Active voice: The car hit the frightened deer. (This sentence emphasizes the car.)

PRACTICE SET 16–4

Directions: Rewrite the following sentences, changing passive voice to active voice.

Example: I was given a watch for my birthday by my parents.

My parents gave me a watch for my birthday.

1. Last week, a rare gemstone was found by the letter carrier.

2. All the hamburgers were eaten by the hungry neighbors.

3. The garden has been weeded and fertilized by Tom.

4. Our large elm tree was struck by lightning.

5. I was given an award for excellence in artistic design.

Some verb pairs create special usage problems.

The verbs *lay/lie*, *set/sit*, and *raise/rise* present special challenges because they are so frequently misused in speech that many writers choose the wrong form. Understanding the difference between transitive and intransitive verbs clears up the confusion.

Form	Transitive (takes a direct object) *to lay:* to put or to place something	Intransitive (does not take a direct object) *to lie:* to recline
Present	lay(s) I lay the book on the desk every day.	lie(s) I lie in bed every day.
Past	laid I laid the book on the desk yesterday.	lay I lay in bed yesterday.
Present participle	laying I am laying the book on the desk now.	lying I am lying in bed now.
Past participle	laid I have laid the book on the desk.	lain I have lain in bed for an hour.

Form	*to set:* to put in a specified place or position	*to sit:* to rest
Present	set(s) He sets the mail on the table every day.	sit(s) He sits in a chair every day.
Past	set He set the mail on the table yesterday.	sat He sat in a chair yesterday.
Present participle	setting He is setting the mail on the table now.	sitting He is sitting in the chair now.
Past participle	set He has set the mail on the table.	sat He has sat in the chair for an hour.

Form	*to raise:* to lift something up	*to rise:* to go up
Present	raise(s) They raise the flag.	rise(s) They rise from their seats.
Past	raised They raised the flag.	rose They rose from their seats.
Present participle	raising They are raising the flag.	rising They are rising from their seats.
Past participle	raised They have raised the flag.	risen They have risen from their seats.

PRACTICE SET 16–5

Directions: Circle the correct verb form in parentheses.

Example: I (lay / laid) on the sofa and watched television.

1. He is (laying / lying) on the floor.

2. The pizza dough has (raised / risen) in the kitchen.

3. The child (set / sat) by her mother's bedside for hours.

4. The potatoes have (laid / lain) in the fields since last week.

5. (Raise / Rise) your hand if you have a question.

6. He (laid / lay) unconscious in the hospital for two weeks.

7. I (set / sat) the notebook on the chair when I arrived.

8. Smoke (raised / rose) from all of the chimneys in the village.

9. Dylan has (laid / lain) the baby in the crib.

10. Let's (lay / lie) out by the pool for the afternoon.

Nouns name persons, places, things, or ideas.

Nouns act as subjects, subject complements, and objects in a sentence. Examine this sentence.

obj. prep.   S   IO   DO   obj. prep.

After the *recital*, the *director* gave *Marcie* a *lecture* about *rudeness*.

In this sentence nouns function as parts of the sentence.

Nouns also can be classified by purpose. The general categories of nouns include common and proper, abstract and concrete, count and noncount, and collective.

Nouns may be either common or proper.

Common nouns usually name a general class (*woman, clerk, mountain, river, house, ship, feelings, autumn*). They do not start with capital letters unless they are the first words of sentences. **Proper nouns** name specific people, places, or things (*Mr. Meyers, Mississippi, Saturday, December, Cheerios, Middle Ages*). They do start with capital letters.

Nouns may be abstract or concrete.

Abstract nouns refer to concepts and ideas that you cannot experience immediately through the senses (*strength, fairness, beauty, diligence, truth*).
Abstract nouns are singular.

Samson's strength was impressive.

Concrete nouns refer to persons, places, or things that you can see, feel, hear, smell, or taste (*books, chair, cake, flowers, smoke, highway*).
Concrete nouns can be singular or plural.

The cake was too sweet.

The chairs need reupholstering.

Nouns may be count or noncount.

As the name implies, **count nouns** refer to persons, places, and things that someone can count (*apples, children, cars, neighbors, laws*).

Categorizing nouns as **count** and **noncount** determines whether or not to use the articles, *a, an,* and *the.*

Use the article *a* or *an* before singular count nouns that are not specific.

> He drove *a truck* in the parade.

(You don't know which truck, so say *a* truck.)

Use the article *the* when you know more specifically which truck.

> We told him to drive *the truck* in the parade.

(Here you have a specific truck in mind, so use *the* truck.)

Noncount nouns name something that is not countable. They are sometimes called mass nouns because they do not consist of individual parts that you can separate and count easily (*dirt, music, flour, labor, pride, housework, sugar, cotton*).

Do not use *a* or *an* before noncount nouns. You would not say the following:

> **Incorrect:**   I put *a sugar* in the cake that I was making.

Often noncount nouns follow words like *some* or *any* that limit or qualify the noun. Look at the following examples:

> I put *some sugar* in the cake that I was making.

> Is there *any pride* in laziness?

Some nouns are collective.

Collective nouns refer to an entire group (*committee, class, choir, family, audience*). They generally take a verb in the singular form. See Chapter 12 for more on collective nouns.

Quick Tip

Nouns can belong to more than one category. For example, nouns like *flour* or *furniture* are concrete, but they also are noncount. *Judgment* is a common noun because it is not capitalized, but it is also an abstract noun because it cannot be experienced through the senses. Categorizing nouns helps in determining capitalization, subject/verb agreement, and article usage.

PRACTICE SET 16–6

Directions: Circle the nouns in the following paragraph.

Water conservation is important to everyone. In September, Mayor Gonzalez asked each citizen to take certain steps to help reduce water use. Turn off the water while you brush your teeth. Use good judgment when you water the lawn. Water no more than once during the week and just in the early morning hours. Finally, run the dishwasher only when it is full. Citizens should mail any other suggestions to the Committee for Water Conservation.

Nouns may have singular or plural forms.

- You can change most nouns from singular to plural by adding -*s* or -*es*.

Singular	Plural
watch	watches
apple	apples
witness	witnesses

- When a singular noun ends in *y* preceded by a consonant, change the *y* to *i* and add -*es* to form the plural.

Singular	Plural
spy	spies
fly	flies
reply	replies

Quick Tip

When a singular noun ends in *y* preceded by a vowel, form the plural by adding -*s* to the word.

Singular	Plural
attorney	attorneys
foray	forays
boy	boys

- Some singular nouns ending in *f* or *fe* form the plural by adding *-s*.

Singular	Plural
cliff	cliffs
chief	chiefs
safe	safes

Others change the *f* or *fe* to *v* and add *-es*.

Singular	Plural
knife	knives
wolf	wolves
thief	thieves

- Singular nouns ending in *o* preceded by a consonant form the plural by adding *-es*.

Singular	Plural
hero	heroes
fresco	frescoes
tomato	tomatoes

- Singular nouns ending in *o* preceded by a vowel form the plural by adding *-s*.

Singular	Plural
radio	radios
cameo	cameos
folio	folios

- Some singular nouns follow rules carried over from Middle English spelling. Note the following irregular plural forms.

Singular	Plural
ox	oxen
deer	deer
woman	women
goose	geese
mouse	mice
child	children
tooth	teeth

Quick Tip

Making the word *woman* plural is especially confusing because in the plural form, the first syllable changes pronunciation, but the second syllable changes spelling. Think about the words *man* and *men*. Then just add *wo-* to them.

| **Singular:** | man | **Plural:** | men |
| **Singular:** | wo–man | **Plural:** | wo–men |

When nouns are compound, as in *mother-in-law* or *maid of honor*, add *-s* to the most important word, which usually comes first.

Singular	**Plural**
mother-in-law	mothers-in-law
attorney general	attorneys general
maid of honor	maids of honor

If you are unsure about how to make a word plural, consult a dictionary.

PRACTICE SET 16–7

Directions: Change the following singular forms into plurals.

Example: woman _____ women _____

1. sister-in-law _____

2. sash _____

3. potato _____

4. fox _____

5. democracy _____

6. rodeo _____

7. donkey _____

8. wife _____

9. window _____

10. sheep _____

Pronouns take the place of nouns.

Pronouns generally refer to nouns called **antecedents,** or words that "go before." The antecedent is the noun that the pronoun replaces.

antecedent   pronoun
Jerome   went home because   he   was sick.

Substituting pronouns for nouns enables writers to avoid repetition.

Repetitious nouns: *Claire* wondered if *Claire* would be able to pull *Claire* together for the debate.

Pronoun substitution: *Claire* wondered if *she* would be able to pull *herself* together for the debate.

Personal pronouns substitute for the nouns naming people, places, things, or ideas.

Personal pronouns take many forms, depending on the gender and number of the antecedent and the specific use of the pronoun in the sentence. They may be masculine, feminine, or neuter; they may be singular or plural; they may be subjective, objective, or possessive case. See Chapter 13 for more explanation of pronoun forms.

The following chart includes all of the personal pronouns.

First Person (the person speaking)

	Singular	Plural
Subjective case	I	we
Objective case	me	us
Possessive case	my, mine	our, ours

Second Person (the person spoken to)

	Singular	Plural
Subjective case	you	you
Objective case	you	you
Possessive case	your, yours	your, yours

Third Person (the person spoken about)

	Singular	Plural
Subjective case	he, she, it	they
Objective case	him, her, it	them
Possessive case	his, her, hers, its	their, theirs

Look at the following sentence:

I gave *him* something that was *theirs.*

This sentence uses three different personal pronouns in three different parts of the sentence. *I* is in the first person singular, subjective case and functions as the subject. *Him* is the third person singular, masculine gender, objective case and functions as the indirect object. *Theirs* is third person plural, possessive case.

PRACTICE SET 16–8

Directions: Fill in the blanks with the appropriate personal pronoun indicated at the end of each sentence.

Example: ___They___ may not like my answer. (third person plural, subjective case)

1. _____ may come to the party without a gift. (second person singular, subjective case)

2. Next week _____ will go with Sascha and Mia to New York. (third person plural, subjective case)

3. Marvin wished _____ would come into the garden again. (third person singular, neuter, subjective case)

4. Please give _____ the ball when you finish. (first person plural, objective case)

5. Tom did his lesson without any help from _____. (third person plural, objective case)

Intensive and reflexive pronouns end in *-self* or *-selves.*

These pronouns include the following:

myself, ourselves, yourself, yourselves, himself, herself, itself, themselves

Intensive pronouns emphasize the nouns they follow by referring to them immediately.

Intensive: The doctor *himself* was surprised at the patient's quick recovery.

Reflexive pronouns point to the subject of the sentence.

Reflexive: The snake sunned *itself* on the rock.

Quick Tip

Speakers and writers sometimes use incorrect forms as reflexive or intensive pronouns. Never use *ourself, hisself, theirself, themselfs,* or *theirselves.* These forms are always incorrect.

Demonstrative pronouns point to, point out, or show something.

This, that, these, and *those* are the common demonstrative pronouns.

This is my new hat.

You must not repeat *that.*

Indefinite pronouns do not refer to particular nouns; rather they are nonspecific.

Here is a list of the most common indefinite pronouns.

Always Singular	Always Plural	Singular or Plural
one, each, another	both	some
either, neither	few	none
everyone, everybody,	several	any
everything	many	all
someone, somebody,		more
something		most
anyone, anybody,		
anything		
no one, nobody,		
nothing		

Anybody can sing.

I told *some* of the children to choose a game.

Interrogative pronouns ask questions.

Common interrogative pronouns are *who, whom, which, what, whose.*

Who are you?

What do you want?

Relative pronouns introduce dependent adjective and noun clauses.

Relative pronouns include *which, whichever, that, who, whoever, whom, whomever, whose, what,* and *whatever.*

Adjective clause: The climber *who crossed the Himalayas* experienced frostbite.

Noun clause: The sponsors offered a reward to *whoever found the missing documents.*

PRACTICE SET 16–9

Directions: Underline the pronouns in the following sentences.

Example: <u>They</u> left for California last night.

1. He can grow beautiful roses, but mine always die.

2. Both of the girls insisted that they try to reach the end of the trail by themselves.

3. I myself am not concerned about hiring anyone for the new position.

4. The diver found the shipwreck although it had been buried for centuries.

5. Who put something in the suggestion box?

Adjectives are words that modify nouns or pronouns.

shiny ring   *blue* sky   *unlikely* hero

Adjectives usually appear immediately before the nouns they describe:

The *night* sky was filled with *bright* stars.

Sometimes, however, adjectives appear in the predicate as subject complements after linking verbs. These are *predicate adjectives.*

The doctor is *busy.*

(*Busy* comes after the linking verb *is* but describes *doctor.*)

Lunch from the restaurant tasted *spicy.*

(*Spicy* modifies *lunch*, but it appears in the predicate after the linking verb *tasted.*)

Specific kinds of adjectives include articles, possessive adjectives, demonstrative adjectives, indefinite adjectives, interrogative adjectives, and proper adjectives.

- **Articles**

   The **articles** *a, an*, and *the* are adjectives. In the phrase *the black cat*, two adjectives modify *cat*. The article *the* limits the cat to a specific one; the adjective *black* describes the cat.

- **Possessives**

   Personal pronouns that show ownership are **possessive adjectives** and always appear before the nouns that they describe. The possessive adjectives include the following: *my, our, your, her, his, its, their.*

   His good reputation made *her* mother happy about *their* relationship.

   Nouns that show ownership also function as adjectives.

   The *horse's* mane was neatly tied in knots.

   Chuck's tuba solo won him first prize.

   See Chapter 11 for information about punctuating possessives.

- **Demonstrative Adjectives**

   Demonstrative adjectives—*this, that, these,* and *those*—identify or point out particular nouns.

   This clue is helping to solve *that* crime.

Quick Tip   Many words function as both adjectives and pronouns or as both adjectives and nouns. Examine a sentence carefully to determine their use. The adjectives come immediately before the noun that they modify. The pronouns and nouns stand alone.

Demonstrative adjective:	*This* day will live in history.
Demonstrative pronoun:	*This* is the day that will live in history.
Indefinite adjective:	*Neither* car has air conditioning.
Indefinite pronoun:	*Neither* of the cars has air conditioning.
Proper adjective:	She speaks the *French* language fluently.
Proper noun:	She speaks *French* fluently.

- **Indefinite Adjectives**

Indefinite adjectives are nonspecific adjectives. They include the following: *another, each, every, either, neither, some, all, any, both, few, several, many, more, most.*

Each child has a distinctive personality.

The English Department is looking for a *few* good professors.

- **Proper Adjectives**

Proper adjectives, which modify nouns, are the names of particular people, places, or things.

You should fly the *American* flag every day.

PRACTICE SET 16–10

Directions: Underline the adjectives in the following sentences and draw arrows to the words they modify.

Example: His primary focus was on that idea.

1. A thin layer of ice gave the Tuscan pines a silvery appearance.

2. A careful observer can see the slightest change in the color of a small chameleon.

3. His happy smile showed that he had received an unexpected surprise.

4. Spectator sports bring in huge crowds at the new stadium.

5. Her expensive luxury car has the latest features.

6. Every picture has the artist's remarkable style crafted into it.

7. The police in riot gear rushed to surround the college campus.

8. The boy's baseball glove needed more padding.

9. Some people dream impossible dreams.

10. Alyssa didn't like either dress in the store window.

Adverbs are words that modify verbs, adjectives, or other adverbs.

The word **adverb** means "to the verb." You might expect adverbs to modify verbs, which they often do, but they also modify adjectives and other adverbs. They answer the questions *where, when, how, why,* and *to what degree.*

Examine the following sentences:

Michael skis *smoothly.* (how?)

Michael skis *daily.* (when?)

Michael skis *here.* (where?)

The adverbs *smoothly, daily,* and *here* all modify the verb *skis,* answering a different question in each sentence.

Adverbs that modify adjectives often tell *how* or *to what degree.*

He took an *extremely* long nap.

(*Extremely* tells *how* about the adjective *long,* which modifies the noun *nap.*)

William is *too* sick to go on the trip.

(*Too* tells *how* about the predicate adjective *sick,* which modifies the noun *William.*)

Adverbs that modify other adverbs tell *to what degree.*

The salesclerk reacted *very* quickly.

(*Very* tells *to what degree* about the adverb *quickly,* which modifies the verb *reacted.*)

Quick Tip

- Many adverbs end in *-ly* (*frequently, really, quickly*), but not all words ending in *-ly* are adverbs. For example, *lovely, likely,* and *lonely* are adjectives.
- The words *not, very, quite,* and *too* are commonly used adverbs.
- Often, you can move adverbs around without significantly changing the meaning of the sentence.

Slowly she answered the question.

She *slowly* answered the question.

She answered the question *slowly.*

PRACTICE SET 16–11

Directions: Underline the adverbs in the following sentences and draw arrows to the words they modify.

Example: Isidoro left the room quietly.

1. Henry has just purchased a fairly expensive computer.

2. Do not take too many chances when you drive at night.

3. Lakeesha recently finished a rather long conversation.

4. Today, my only friend moved away.

5. Never swim alone at night.

6. She simply let her hair dry naturally.

7. Marilyn Monroe had a very sad life.

8. I would also like to come home early tonight.

9. A person can be quite lonely in a crowded room.

10. Speak softly, but carry a big stick.

Adjectives and adverbs show degrees of comparison.

Words in the positive degree make no comparison. They simply modify.

The *bright* light from the helicopter shone onto the sidewalk.

The fisherman dove *rapidly* into the water to save the child.

A *foolish* decision can create a lifetime of regret.

Words in the comparative degree compare two things.

The light from the helicopter was *brighter* than the light from the searchlight.

The fisherman swam *more rapidly* than the lifeguard.

I realize that my choice to sleep was *more foolish* than your decision to study.

Words in the superlative degree compare more than two things.

The light from the helicopter was the *brightest* of all the lights at the scene of the accident.

Of the three swimmers who were trying to save the child, the fisherman swam the *most rapidly.*

Choosing to sleep rather than study was the *most foolish* decision that I have ever made.

Adjectives and adverbs form the comparative and superlative degrees in three ways.

1. For most one- and two-syllable adjectives and some short adverbs, add *-er* for comparatives and *-est* for superlatives. For two-syllable adjectives ending in a consonant followed by a *y*, change the *y* to *i*, and add *-er* or *-est*.

Base Form	**Comparative**	**Superlative**
long	longer	longest
near	nearer	nearest
fast	faster	fastest
easy	easier	easiest
dirty	dirtier	dirtiest

2. For adjectives of three or more syllables and most adverbs, especially those ending in *-ly*, add *more* and *most* or *less* and *least* to make the comparative or superlative forms.

Base Form	**Comparative**	**Superlative**
persuasive	more persuasive	most persuasive
important	more important	most important
slowly	less slowly	least slowly
beautiful	more beautiful	most beautiful
diligent	less diligent	least diligent
quickly	less quickly	least quickly

3. Some adjectives and adverbs have irregular comparative and superlative forms.

Base Form	**Comparative**	**Superlative**
good	better	best
well	better	best
bad	worse	worst
badly	worse	worst
much	more	most
many	more	most

   James is a *bad* driver.

   Jeremy is a *worse* driver than James.

   Joseph is the *worst* driver of the three.

Quick Tip

Good and *well* are frequently misused. *Good* is always an adjective. *Well* is an adjective when it means healthy and an adverb when it tells how something is done.

Incorrect:	I did *good* on my test.
Correct:	I did *well* on my test.

Bad and *badly* are also frequently misused. *Bad* is an adjective, so it should follow a linking verb.

Incorrect:	I feel *badly* about your loss.
Correct:	I feel *bad* about your loss.

Do not use *more* or *most* and the *-er* or *-est* endings in the same comparison.

Incorrect:	Atlantis was *more richer* in art than historians once believed.
Correct:	Atlantis was *richer* in art than historians once believed.

Make sure that all comparisons are complete.

Incorrect:	The gold in the antique necklace seems shinier.
Complete:	The gold in the antique necklace seems shinier than the gold in my necklace.

Incorrect:	My solo got a higher rating than Margo.
Complete:	My solo got a higher rating than Margo's solo.

Do not use the superlative form when comparing two things.

Incorrect:	Between the two of us, who is the strongest?
Correct:	Between the two of us, who is stronger?

Do not confuse adjective and adverb forms in comparison.

Incorrect:	Your car runs smoother than mine.
Correct:	Your car runs more smoothly than mine.

PRACTICE SET 16–12

Directions: Rewrite the following sentences, correcting any errors in comparison.

Example: This is the more exciting of the three novels.

This is the most exciting of the three novels.

1. Dru was the better runner on her track team.

2. The light from the comet was the most clear in the night sky.

3. I like lobster better.

4. Victoria is the smartest of the twins.

5. Nathan ran quicker than Noah.

6. Of Los Angeles and New York, I like New York best.

7. She was the worst of the two spellers.

8. Among Josie, Angelina, and Sally, Josie is the taller.

9. A bassoon's tone is deeper than an oboe.

10. My new computer responds slower than my old one.

Prepositions connect nouns or pronouns to a sentence by forming groups of words called prepositional phrases.

Prepositions are usually just one word, but sometimes a group of words can act as a preposition. These groups of words are **phrasal prepositions** or **prepositional expressions.**

about	beneath	in case of	since
above	beside	in front of	through
according to	between	in spite of	throughout
across	beyond	inside	to
after	but (meaning *except*)	into	toward
against	by	like	under
along	by way of	near	underneath
along with	concerning	of	until
among	despite	off	up
around	down	on	up to
as	during	onto	upon
as well as	except	out	with
at	for	out of	with reference to
because of	from	outside	with regard to
before	in	over	with the exception of
behind	in addition to	past	within
below	in back of	regarding	without

A noun or pronoun connected to a sentence by a preposition is the **object of the preposition.** Prepositional phrases always modify.

     prep.   obj. of the prep.   prep.   obj. of the prep.
They walked *along the riverbank* and talked *about many issues.*

prep.   obj. of the prep.   prep.   obj. of the prep.

The contractor left the pile *of*   *lumber*   *in front of the*   *door.*

A preposition may have a compound object.

prep. obj. of the prep.

We gave the party *for* *Thad and Michelle.*

PRACTICE SET 16–13

Directions: Underline the prepositions in the following sentences. Then put the entire prepositional phrase in parentheses.

Example: We sang (<u>for</u> our supper).

1. A swarm of bees outside the house gathered pollen from the flowers.

2. Seeing snow on the street in the middle of April was odd.

3. In the forest of pines by the lake, we had our picnic.

4. According to legend, a knight rides through these woods at dusk.

5. Aesop wrote a fable about a fox and some grapes.

Conjunctions connect parts of sentences, often showing the relationship of particular words, phrases, and clauses to the rest of the sentence.

Conjunctions may be coordinating, subordinating, or correlative.

Coordinating conjunctions connect words, phrases, or clauses of equal rank.

And, but, or, nor, for, so, and *yet* are the coordinating conjunctions.

adj.   adj.

Joining two words: Alex was industrious *and* smart.

prep. phrase

Joining two phrases: The lost contact lens must be in the drain *or*

prep. phrase

in the vacuum cleaner.

IC   IC

Joining two clauses: I can come to the dinner party, *but* I cannot stay late.

Subordinating conjunctions introduce dependent clauses, called subordinate clauses, and connect them to the independent clauses of sentences.

The following is a list of the most common subordinating conjunctions:

after	even if	though
although	even though	unless
as	if	until
as if	since	when
as though	so that	whenever
because	than	where
before	that	while

SC
When the mega-mall opened, the smaller shopping center closed.

                              SC
The pioneers traveled *where* no one had explored.

SC
If I want to finish the project, I will have to work during the weekend.

Correlative conjunctions appear in pairs and join elements that are parallel in structure. Correlative conjunctions include the following: *both/and, either/or, neither/nor, not only/but also, whether/or.*

Neither Madison *nor* Holly took enough money to the garage sale.

(correlative conjunctions connecting the nouns *Madison* and *Holly*)

She *not only* wrote to the governor *but also* circulated a petition among her neighbors.

(correlative conjunctions connecting the verbs *wrote* and *circulated*)

Whether skiing *or* snowboarding, you should always check your equipment.

(correlative conjunctions connecting the gerunds *skiing* and *snowboarding*)

PRACTICE SET 16–14

Directions: Underline any conjunctions in the sentences below and label them as coordinating, subordinating, or correlative.

                    subordinating   *coordinating*
Example: Before   I left home, I packed my bags   and   paid my bills.

1. Not only department stores but also specialty shops are coming to the new International Plaza.

2. Missy always walked to work because she wanted to get some exercise.

3. The back seat of my car was soaked, for I had left my windows open.

4. While the cat is away, the mice will play.

5. She did not eat any breakfast, so she ate a hearty lunch.

Quick Tip

Prepositions, conjunctions, adverbs, and infinitives sometimes look alike.

Preposition: *After* the game, we saw a movie.

Subordinating conjunction: *After* we left the game, we saw a movie.

Preposition: He bought a gift *for* her birthday.

Coordinating conjunction: He bought a gift, *for* his wife's birthday was Saturday.

Preposition: The mouse crawled *inside* the box.

Adverb: The mouse crawled *inside*.

Preposition: I went *to* the shop.

Infinitive: I like *to shop*.

PRACTICE SET 16–15

Directions: In the sentences below, label the words in boldface as prepositions, conjunctions, infinitives, or adverbs.

Example: Everyone **but** Brandon stayed to work, **but** we still didn't meet our deadline.
(prep. / conjunction)

1. He traveled **to** China **to do** research for his dissertation.

2. The rain came **down** heavily as we walked **down** the street.

3. I placed the gift **before** her **before** she left the party.

4. **Until** I gave her an alarm clock, she always slept **until** noon.

5. **To stay** physically fit, you must go **to** the gym.

Conjunctive adverbs join independent clauses.

Below is a list of some common conjunctive adverbs.

consequently   however   similarly
finally   moreover   then
furthermore   nevertheless   therefore
hence   next   thus

Using different methods to join clauses provides variety to your writing. The three sentences below say the same thing but in different ways:

Coordinating conjunction: We will work together, *and* we will accomplish the task.

Subordinating conjunction: *When* we work together, we will accomplish the task.

Conjunctive adverb: We will work together; *consequently*, we will accomplish the task.

Quick Tip

Both conjunctive adverbs and coordinating conjunctions join closely related independent clauses; however, it is important to note how punctuation differs with their use. A comma separates independent clauses joined by a co-ordinating conjunction. Remember to place the comma before the conjunction, not after it.

I need a new car, but I don't have the money to buy one.

A semicolon separates independent clauses joined by a conjunctive adverb. Place a comma after the conjunctive adverb.

I need a new car; however, I don't have the money to buy one.

Using a comma to separate independent clauses joined by a conjunctive adverb creates a comma splice, a type of run-on sentence.

Incorrect: I need a new car, however, I don't have the money to buy one.

See Chapter 9 for more on run-on sentences.

Interjections are words that show surprise or strong feeling and are not grammatically connected to the sentence.

Commas follow mild interjections; exclamation points follow strong interjections.

Oh, I understand what you are saying.

Wow! I am finally finished with this chapter.

COMPOSITION WARM-UP

Directions: In the paragraph below, write the part of speech above the words in boldface.

Brimming with Old World charm, the **medieval** city of Rothenburg **attracts** thousands **of** vacationers every year. **It** is located in the foothills of the **lush** Austrian Alps. Visitors love the **beautiful** setting **that** this small city shares with the surrounding countryside. **They** enjoy the crumbling **castle** walls, wood footbridges, and **winding** stone roads. A **most** charming part of the city is the shopping district, **which** is built **around** a *Platz*, or town square. **Here** tradesmen from **cooks** to watchmakers create **their** wares and peddle them on the streets and in the quaint shops. **The** shopkeepers live in narrow townhouses decorated with flower-filled window boxes **and** red-tiled roofs. **Perhaps** the most attractive aspect of **Rothenburg** is the stone wall that **completely** surrounds the city. Tourists gather **early** in the morning **so that** they **can climb** the wall and make a one-mile trek. The top of the wall gives the hikers a clear **view** of the red roofs, splendid gardens, and neat **but** unmatched houses. **Oh,** what a world of fantasy greets the traveler in this special city!

COMPOSITION PRACTICE

Directions: Write your own sentences using the parts of speech indicated below. Use the dictionary to help you.

1. Use *down* as a preposition.

2. Use *down* as an adverb.

3. Use *well* as a noun.

4. Use *well* as an adverb.

5. Use *like* as a preposition.

6. Use *like* as a verb.

7. Use *morning* as an adjective.

8. Use *morning* as a noun.

9. Use *brown* as a verb.

10. Use *brown* as an adjective.

Selected Answers
to Chapter Exercises

Chapter 1

Test Yourself

```
     pn    adv       v   prep adj   n
1. He strongly objected to   the idea.
```

```
   adj    n      v    adj  n  prep adj    n
2. A neighbor raked the yard after the storm.
```

```
             n       adv     v   prep adj  n  prep    n
3. Mrs. Stanton often thought of   a   visit to Germany.
```

```
        pn     v     v  prep adj   n  prep adj     n
4. Anyone may come to   the party for the mayor.
```

```
     adj    n     v    v   adj   n
5. All persons must obey the law.
```

```
   adj   noun      v      prep  n
6. A friendship evolved over time.
```

```
     adj  adj     n   prep adj     n      v   pn
7. The first speaker on the program was she.
```

```
         n      v    adv prep adj    n
8. Mushrooms grow mostly in dark caves.
```

```
         n     conj    n     v   adj adj    n
9. Fishermen and sailors know the sea currents.
```

```
      n    v    prep adj  adj     n    adj     n
10. Mort goes through a precise ritual every morning.
```

Chapter 2

Test Yourself

1. S/V/IO/DO
2. S/LV/SC
3. S/V/DO
4. S/V/DO/OC
5. S/V/DO
6. S/V
7. S/V/SO/OC
8. S/V/IO/DO
9. S/LV/SC
10. S/LV/SC

Word Watchers Practice Set

1. affect
2. among
3. capital
4. except
5. chose
6. capitol
7. accept
8. effect
9. choose
10. between

Chapter 3

Test Yourself

    adj   adv   adv   adj
1. Great apes live peacefully in completely protected areas.

    adj   adv   adj adj
2. His car skidded sharply into the wrong lane.

     adj   adv adj   adv   adj adv adj   adj
3. Mark's sister was so happy that she finally got a very high raise in her salary.

      adv   adj   adj adj   adj adj
4. Yesterday, my friend found a unique stamp for her new collection.

    adj   adv   adj   adv adj   adj
5. The messengers quickly recognized that most people were not ready for bad news.

    adj   adj   adv   adj   adj
6. The proud winner immediately ran to the nearest telephone.

      adj   adj   adj   adj   adj
7. In modern communication, short, concise e-mails have replaced long, wordy letters.

      adv   adj adj   adj adv adj
8. We never consider the serious consequences when we make a too hasty decision.

       adv   adj   adj adj
9. One should always allow for some mistakes in a bank account.

    adj   adj   adv   adj adj
10. The seaside community had not expected a high tide.

Word Watchers Practice Set

1. continuous
2. further
3. site
4. complemented
5. immigrated
6. farther
7. continual
8. cited
9. compliment
10. emigrated

Chapter 4

Test Yourself

1. prepositional phrase
2. appositive
3. prepositional phrase
4. prepositional phrase
5. verb phrase
6. verb phrase
7. appositive
8. prepositional phrase
9. verb phrase
10. prepositional phrase

Word Watchers Practice Set

1. lose
2. led
3. number
4. passed
5. fewer
6. loose
7. fewer
8. lead
9. past
10. lead

Chapter 5

Test Yourself

1.   *participle*   *participle*
   Anticipating an accident, he swerved away from the approaching car.

2.   *participle*   *infinitive*   *infinitive*
   My pressing dilemma is whether to sign the contract now or to wait until next year.

3.   *participle*   *participle*
   The swollen river rose two feet a day, overflowing its banks.

4.   *participle*   *infinitive*
   Exhausted from the drive, the college student decided to stop at a motel.

5.   *gerund*   *participle*
   Mastering the game of chess takes hours of concentrated effort.

6.   *participle*   *infinitive*
   Her accumulated wealth increased her ability to help needy children.

7.   *gerund*   *participle*
   Singing arias gave the trained tenor the practice that he needed.

8. Eating healthy foods can lead to a prolonged life.
   gerund (Eating healthy foods)   participle (prolonged)

9. Avoiding tobacco and alcohol improved his condition.
   gerund (Avoiding tobacco and alcohol)

10. Avoiding tobacco and alcohol, he was able to improve his condition.
   participle (Avoiding tobacco and alcohol)

Word Watchers Practice Set

1. stationary
2. too
3. than
4. principal
5. whether
6. principles
7. too
8. principal
9. stationery
10. principles

Chapter 6

Test Yourself

1. (You) Never leave the dryer running when you are not at home.

2. Will Karen find the message on her bulletin board?

3. Why did Josef cancel his flight?

4. There are no limes on the tree.

5. (You) Offer your enemies your hand in friendship.

6. (You) Please do not leave your station unattended.

7. There is only one reason for the delay.

8. How do these photographs compare with the ones from last week?

9. Should we taste the sauce before serving it?

10. (You) Tell me the truth.

Word Watchers Practice Set

(Answers may vary.)

1. They have been dating since July.
2. She is two months pregnant.
3. I'm anxious to meet the drummer.

4. I hope that the baby will sleep so I can watch the basketball game.
5. ... warm clothing, blankets, etc.
6. ... she could not have cared less.
7. Today, it is important ...
8. Markie ... told his mother that he was very hungry.
9. This strange bird is unique.
10. She was very casual in her attitude.

Chapter 7

Test Yourself

1. what you are saying—noun clause
2. When Woodstock drew to a close in 1969—adverb clause
3. that shed their leaves before the cold or dry season—adjective clause
4. because McClellan would not send the troops into battle—adverb clause
5. which took place on April 17, 1961—adjective clause
6. whoever was making the racket—noun clause
7. where I am going—noun clause
8. Where you live—noun clause   that you should purchase—adjective clause
9. where the accident occurred—adjective clause
10. wherever you go—adverb clause

Word Watchers Practice Set

1. green
2. moved
3. met
4. linked
5. if possible
6. consensus
7. announced
8. concluded
9. always
10. stopped

Chapter 8

Test Yourself

1. simple
2. complex
3. complex
4. compound
5. compound-complex
6. simple
7. compound-complex
8. complex
9. compound-complex
10. simple

Word Watchers Practice Set

1. congradulated = congratulated
2. writting = writing
3. alot = a lot
4. inconvience = inconvenience
5. athelete = athlete

Chapter 9

Test Yourself

1. F	6. RS
2. F	7. F
3. C	8. C
4. RS	9. RS
5. F	10. F

Word Watchers Practice Set

1. judgement = judgment
2. definately = definitely
3. lisence = license
4. occassion = occasion
5. develope = develop   seperate = separate

Chapter 10

Test Yourself

1. Carole ordered sheets, towels, and blankets from the discount catalog.

2. correct

3. Even though the cook followed the recipe exactly, the cake was dry and tasteless.

4. Eric received an MP3 player, not a laptop computer, from his grandparents for his birthday.

5. The toddler is very tired, but she refuses to take a nap.

6. To win the election, each candidate spent millions of dollars on television advertising.

7. The protesters marched without a permit and were, therefore, arrested by the police.

8. correct

9. *Law and Order,* my father's favorite television show, presents fictional stories based on real-life crimes.

10. On October 4, 2005, Gina Calhoun, M.D., opened a plastic surgery clinic in Athens, Georgia.

Word Watchers Practice Set

1. regardless	3. themselves
2. would have could have	4. supposed

5. anywhere
6. should have
7. Nowhere
8. himself
9. used
10. themselves

Chapter 11

Test Yourself

1. hours; then *or* hours. Then
2. *Romeo and Juliet or* <u>Romeo and Juliet</u>
3. cheese—these
4. economics
5. its
6. such as batteries,
7. reading.
8. soon?" Max
9. "Theme for English B"
10. men's

Word Watchers Practice Set

1. It's
2. which
3. who's
4. There
5. you're
6. who
7. their
8. its
9. whose
10. They're

Chapter 12

Test Yourself

1. was
2. are
3. celebrates
4. comes
5. needs
6. is
7. brings
8. contain
9. has
10. appears

Word Watchers Practice Set

1. different from
2. well
3. to
4. bad
5. as
6. badly
7. surely
8. like
9. well
10. to

Chapter 13

Test Yourself

1. its		6. I	
2. their		7. His	
3. its		8. her	
4. her		9. whom	
5. we		10. who	

Word Watchers Practice Set

(Answers may vary.)

1. casual
2. guys, fellows, boys, men
3. among
4. First
5. permitted, allowed, acceptable

6. ignored, disrespected
7. man
8. 24 hours a day, around the clock
9. my error, my mistake
10. unusual, strange

Chapter 14

Test Yourself

1. The victim he was sadly comforting told him what had happened.
   The victim he was comforting told him sadly what had happened.
   Sadly, the victim he was comforting told him what had happened.
2. Chris ate the chicken while he was shopping at the mall.
3. Kevin drinks orange juice every morning even though he hates it.
   Even though he hates it, Kevin drinks orange juice every morning.
4. Rover happily began to wag his tail.
   Rover began to wag his tail happily.
   Happily, Rover began to wag his tail.
5. While the technicians were installing the software, a power surge destroyed the computer's operating system.
6. correct
7. People who do not like hamburgers can now get salads at fast-food restaurants.
8. Lauren said Don was late to work frequently.
   Lauren frequently said Don was late to work.
9. While I was climbing out of the bathtub, the washcloth fell on the floor.
10. I buy only fresh fruit.

Word Watchers Practice Set

(Answers may vary.)

1. someone may do the same for me someday
2. books
3. I won't know until the instructor returns the test
4. she will be able to afford it
5. I gave up trying to discipline them
6. all actions have consequences
7. The party had a well-known band and delicious food, but Ruben did not enjoy himself.
8. he will probably find a better one
9. eat low-calorie foods and exercise every day
10. good-looking people do not always make good mates

Chapter 15

Test Yourself

(Answers may vary.)

1. When you have a cold, you should drink plenty of fluids.
2. He ate everything in sight and then said that he was still hungry.
3. Eating oatmeal will lower your cholesterol.
4. The coach said that he was finished and asked for any questions.
5. He is as funny as if not funnier than David Letterman.
6. Eating properly, exercising consistently, and sleeping soundly are three requirements of good health.
7. Your not being able to swim doesn't mean we can't go to the beach.
8. He impressed her because he is a doctor.
9. In order to make the soup, Jessica placed a chicken in the pot.
10. The expensive fabric that she bought made beautiful curtains.

Word Watchers Practice Set

(Answers may vary.)

1. server (not waiter)
2. all voters should bring their registration cards
3. firefighters (not firemen)
4. humankind (not mankind)
5. flight attendants (not stewardesses)
6. people in business (not businessmen)
7. chairs or chairpersons (not chairmen)
8. spouses, partners, guests (not wives)
9. synthetic (not manmade)
10. the talent of the workers

Index